"A wonderful, inspiring book. These meditations lead us to genuine, uplifting prayer. In a magical chemistry, we are led to know better both God and John XXIII." **Timothy E. O'Connell,** author, *Tend Your Own Garden: How to Raise Great Kids* and *Good People, Tough Choices*

"Huebsch has done a masterful job of using biography as a bridge to spirituality; of pressing one man's biographical truth into the service of universal love. This book will be dog-eared from use." **Joseph Roccasalvo,** Center for the Study of World Religions, and author of *Portrait of a Woman: A Novel*

"The content and style of this book reflect the charm, humor, and global vision of a man whose life was rooted in faith. One again breathes the fresh air of Pope John's vitality and accessibility in the 'commonness' of his spirituality." **Camilla Burns,** SND de N, PhD, director, Institute of Pastoral Studies, Loyola University, Chicago

✧ *Companions for the Journey* ✧

Praying with
Pope John XXIII

✧ *Companions for the Journey* ✧

Praying with
Pope John XXIII

by
Bill Huebsch

Saint Mary's Press
Christian Brothers Publications
Winona, Minnesota

The publishing team included Michael Wilt, development editor; Laurie A. Berg, copy editor; James H. Gurley, production editor; Laurie Geisler, cover designer; Sam Thiewes, illustrator; pre-press, printing, and binding by the graphics division of Saint Mary's Press.

The psalms in this book are from *Psalms Anew: In Inclusive Language,* compiled by Nancy Schreck and Maureen Leach (Winona, MN: Saint Mary's Press, 1986). Copyright © 1986 by Saint Mary's Press. All rights reserved.

All other scriptural quotations in this book are from the New Revised Standard Version of the Bible. Copyright © 1989 by the Division of Christian Education of the National Council of Churches of Christ in the United States of America. All rights reserved.

Printed in the United States of America

Printing: 9 8 7 6 5 4 3 2 1

Year: 2007 06 05 04 03 02 01 00 99

ISBN 0-88489-596-3

Genuine recycled paper with 10% post-consumer waste.
Printed with soy-based ink.

✧ Contents ✧

Foreword   9

Introduction   15

Meditations

1. **Forgetting Oneself**   31
2. **Charity Above All Else**   36
3. **Do Not Eat Alone**   42
4. **Seek Peace and Follow After It**   48
5. **An Ecumenical Spirit**   55
6. **More Than Merely Christian**   61
7. **Open Wide Your Arms to All**   67
8. **Don't Take Yourself Too Seriously**   73
9. **Living by What We Preach**   79
10. **Holy Optimism**   84
11. **Simplicity of Heart and Speech**   89
12. **Read Little but Well**   94
13. **Die Well**   100
14. **Holy Folly**   107
15. **Youthfulness of Spirit**   113

✧ Foreword ✧

Companions for the Journey

Just as food is required for human life, so are companions. Indeed, the word *companions* comes from two Latin words: *com,* meaning "with," and *panis,* meaning "bread." Companions nourish our heart, mind, soul, and body. They are also the people with whom we can celebrate the sharing of bread.

Perhaps the most touching stories in the Bible are about companionship: the Last Supper, the wedding feast at Cana, the sharing of the loaves and the fishes, and Jesus' breaking of bread with the disciples on the road to Emmaus. Each incident of companionship with Jesus revealed more about his mercy, love, wisdom, suffering, and hope. When Jesus went to pray in the Garden of Olives, he craved the companionship of the Apostles. They let him down. But God sent the Spirit to inflame the hearts of the Apostles, and they became faithful companions to Jesus and to one another.

Throughout history, other faithful companions have followed Jesus and the Apostles. These saints and mystics have also taken the journey from conversion, through suffering, to resurrection. Just as they were inspired by the holy people who went before them, so too may you be inspired by these saints and mystics and take them as your companions on your spiritual journey.

The Companions for the Journey series is a response to the spiritual hunger of Christians. This series makes available the rich spiritual teachings of mystics and guides whose wisdom can help us on our pilgrimage. As you complete the last meditation in each volume, it is hoped that you will feel supported, challenged, and affirmed by a soul-companion on your spiritual journey.

The spiritual hunger that has emerged over the last twenty years is a great sign of renewal in Christian life. People fill retreat programs and workshops on topics in spirituality. The demand for spiritual directors exceeds the number available. Interest in the lives and writings of saints and mystics is increasing as people search for models of whole and holy Christian life.

Praying with Pope John XXIII

Praying with Pope John XXIII is more than just a book about Pope John's spirituality. This book seeks to engage you in praying in the way that Pope John did about issues and themes that were central to his experience. Each meditation can enlighten your understanding of his spirituality and lead you to reflect on your own experience.

The goal of *Praying with Pope John XXIII* is that you will discover Pope John's rich spirituality and integrate his spirit and wisdom into your relationship with God, with your brothers and sisters, and with your own heart and mind.

Suggestions for Praying with Pope John XXIII

Meet Pope John XXIII, a fascinating companion for your pilgrimage, by reading the introduction to this book. It provides a brief biography of Pope John and an outline of the major themes of his spirituality.

Once you meet Pope John, you will be ready to pray with him and to encounter God, your sisters and brothers, and yourself in new and wonderful ways. To help your prayer, here are some suggestions that have been part of the tradition of Christian spirituality:

Create a sacred space. Jesus said, "Whenever you pray, go into your room and shut the door and pray to your [God] who is in secret; and your [God] who sees in secret will reward you" (Matthew 6:6). Solitary prayer is best done in a place where you can have privacy and silence, both of which can be luxuries in the life of busy people. If privacy and silence are not possible, create a quiet, safe place within yourself, perhaps while riding to and from work, while sitting in line at the dentist's office, or while waiting for someone. Do the best you can, knowing that a loving God is present everywhere. Whether the meditations in this book are used for solitary prayer or with a group, try to create a prayerful mood with candles, meditative music, an open Bible, or a crucifix.

Open yourself to the power of prayer. Every human experience has a religious dimension. All of life is suffused with God's presence. So remind yourself that God is present as you begin your period of prayer. Do not worry about distractions. If something keeps intruding during your prayer, spend some time talking with God about it. Be flexible because God's spirit blows where it will.

Prayer can open your mind and widen your vision. Be open to new ways of seeing God, people, and yourself. As you open yourself to the spirit of God, different emotions are evoked, such as sadness from tender memories, or joy from a celebration recalled. Our emotions are messages from God that can tell us much about our spiritual quest. Also, prayer strengthens our will to act. Through prayer, God can touch our will and empower us to live according to what we know is true.

Finally, many of the meditations in this book will call you to employ your memories, your imagination, and the circumstances of your life as subjects for prayer. The great mystics and saints realized that they had to use all their resources to know God better. Indeed, God speaks to us continually and touches us constantly. We must learn to listen and feel with all the means that God has given us.

Come to prayer with an open mind, heart, and will.

Preview each meditation before beginning. After you have placed yourself in God's presence, spend a few moments previewing the readings and especially the reflection activities. Several reflection activities are given in each meditation because different styles of prayer appeal to different personalities

or personal needs. **Note that each meditation has more reflection activities than can be done during one prayer period.
Therefore, select only one or two reflection activities each
time you use a meditation. Do not feel compelled to complete all the reflection activities.**

Read meditatively. Each meditation offers you a story
about Pope John and a reading from his writings. Take your
time reading. If a particular phrase touches you, stay with it.
Relish its feelings, meanings, and concerns.

Use the reflections. Following the readings is a short reflection in commentary form, which is meant to give perspective to the readings. Then you are offered several ways of
meditating on the readings and the theme of the prayer. You
may be familiar with the different methods of meditating, but
in case you are not, they are described briefly here:

✦ *Repeated short prayer or mantra:* One means of focusing your
   prayer is to use a *mantra,* or "prayer word." The mantra
   may be a single word or a short phrase taken from the
   readings or from the Scriptures. For example, a short
   prayer for meditation 13 in this book might simply be
   "I am here, God." Repeated slowly in harmony with your
   breathing, the mantra helps you center your heart and
   mind on one action or attribute of God.

✦ *Lectio divina:* This type of meditation is "divine studying,"
   a concentrated reflection on the word of God or the wisdom of a spiritual writer. Most often in *lectio divina,* you
   will be invited to read one of the passages several times
   and then concentrate on one or two sentences, pondering
   their meaning for you and their effect on you. *Lectio divina*
   commonly ends with formulation of a resolution.

✦ *Guided meditation:* In this type of meditation, our imagination helps us consider alternative actions and likely conse-
   quences. Our imagination helps us experience new ways of
   seeing God, our neighbors, ourselves, and nature. When
   Jesus told his followers parables and stories, he engaged
   their imagination. In this book, you will be invited to follow
   guided meditations.

One way of doing a guided meditation is to read the scene or story several times, until you know the outline and can recall it when you enter into reflection. Or before your prayer time, you may wish to record the meditation on a tape recorder. If so, remember to allow pauses for reflection between phrases and to speak with a slow, peaceful pace and tone. Then, during prayer, when you have finished the readings and the reflection commentary, you can turn on your recording of the meditation and be led through it. If you find your own voice too distracting, ask a friend to make the tape for you.

✦ *Examen of consciousness:* The reflections often will ask you to examine how God has been speaking to you in your past and present experience—in other words, the reflections will ask you to examine your awareness of God's presence in your life.

✦ *Journal writing:* Writing is a process of discovery. If you write for any length of time, stating honestly what is on your mind and in your heart, you will unearth much about who you are, how you stand with your God, what deep longings reside in your soul, and more. In some reflections, you will be asked to write a dialog with Jesus or someone else. If you have never used writing as a means of meditation, try it. Reserve a special notebook for your journal writing. If desired, you can go back to your entries at a future time for an examen of consciousness.

✦ *Action:* Occasionally, a reflection will suggest singing a favorite hymn, going out for a walk, or undertaking some other physical activity. Actions can be meaningful forms of prayer.

Using the Meditations for Group Prayer

If you wish to use the meditations for community prayer, these suggestions may help:

✦ Read the theme to the group. Call the community into the presence of God, using the short opening prayer. Invite one or two participants to read one or both readings. If you use both readings, observe the pause between them.

✦ The reflection commentary may be used as a reading, or it can be deleted, depending on the needs and interests of the group.

✦ Select one of the reflection activities for your group. Allow sufficient time for your group to reflect, to recite a centering prayer or mantra, to accomplish a studying prayer *(lectio divina)*, or to finish an examen of consciousness. Depending on the group and the amount of available time, you may want to invite the participants to share their reflections, responses, or petitions with the group.

✦ Reading the passage from the Scriptures may serve as a summary of the meditation.

✦ If a formulated prayer or a psalm is given as a closing, it may be recited by the entire group. Or you may ask participants to offer their own prayers for the closing.

Now you are ready to begin praying with Pope John XXIII, a faithful and caring companion on this stage of your spiritual journey. It is hoped that you will find him to be a true soul-companion.

CARL KOCH
Series Editor

✧ Introduction ✧

Impressions

Some writers and biographers have created the impression that Pope John XXIII was a simple peasant priest, raised suddenly and without preparation to the papacy. The impression continues that once John became pope, he was so naive about church politics and history that he summoned an ecumenical council of the church, unaware of what its outcome might be. Some have even thought of him as an innocent but bumbling fellow, out of touch with protocol and tradition.

It is more accurate, however, to recognize that Pope John XXIII knew precisely who he was and what he was doing. From his earliest days, he cultivated a cheerful but powerful spirituality that tied him intimately to Christ and allowed him to trust the impulses of the Holy Spirit as they arose in his heart. And as for the Second Vatican Council, in which he convened the Roman Catholic bishops, we can now see that the times called for this council and that Pope John's entire life prepared him to convene, organize, and host it.

But the key to understanding Pope John is his faith. Indeed, it is safe to say that everything in his life was driven by that. It radiated in his home. It motivated his decision to enter the priesthood. It allowed him to humbly accept assignment after assignment, even though not all of them were as he would have liked them to be. Faith was the single factor that allowed him to accept his election to the papacy. Once there, faith caused him to open his arms, and, like Christ, accept and love women and men the world over. Faith gave him the courage to summon a council of the Catholic church and to invite members of other denominations to observe the council. It gave him the courage to join in dialog with the Jews, and to express love and concern for all people, even those who believe in no god at all. Faith drove him to call forcefully for world peace and disarmament. And faith led him to a profoundly peaceful and ecumenical death—Pope John XXIII was mourned the world over, having touched the lives of people of all denominations and religions.

Pope John had faith. He had faith in the church, a common enough phenomenon in the pre–Vatican II period of Catholic history. But more important, he had faith in Christ, who is beyond the church. This wider faith in Christ allowed Pope John to see the church with a fresh perspective and with enough distance that he could judge it according to the Gospel and call it to renewal.

Pope John's journey of faith is recorded in his journal, but simply reading his journal does not provide the reader with enough information to understand him. He was such a profoundly social person that we must also read what eyewitnesses to his life had to say. In such accounts we find a generous spirit, a warm wit, a commonness that put on no airs, and a welcoming hand. Pope John often touched those with whom he spoke, physically touched them, communicating his generous love for them.

Coming to know Pope John XXIII can be a life-changing experience. He is a vibrant model of the church and its teachings.

Roots

Pope John XXIII did indeed begin his life as a peasant. He was born Angelo Giuseppe Roncalli in northern Italy on 25 November 1881, at the home of his parents. Giovanni Battista Roncalli and Marianna Mazzola Roncalli lived in the village of Sotto il Monte, ten miles from Bergamo. Theirs was a very large family of farmers, and Angelo often said later in life that he had come into the world in poverty and would leave it in the same way. He was baptized before the end of his first day of life, at the insistence of his godfather and great uncle, Zaverio. There was no special celebration other than a glass of wine for the adults.

Angelo was reared in the open fields and hillsides of Bergamo, working with his father alongside many other members of his family. He always remained tied to his home region. When he was ready to start school, he showed immediate promise. Before Angelo was ten, he had been confirmed and had received his first Communion. Neither sacrament was accompanied by a special celebration. They were an expected part of life and were done simply.

Roncalli's background in Sotto il Monte provided him with the values that he carried into the papacy. In Sotto il Monte, life was lived without conflict between nature and grace. The two were inseparable. The rhythms of life and of the church wound around one another intimately. The values of Christ and his Mother dominated their lives: no stranger was ever turned away, despite their own poverty, and always strangers were received in the name of Christ. Personal sacrifice, humility, acceptance of life as it unfolded before him, a deep trust in providence, and a cheerful spirit—these were all integral parts of Roncalli's life from the very beginning.

Seminary Days

The young Roncalli entered the seminary in nearby Bergamo in 1895 and pursued his studies there until 1900. During this period, in 1896, he began writing a journal, a practice he continued throughout his life. Roncalli's seminary years were formative for him. The entries in his journal during these years reveal a cheerful but serious student, concerned with growing in the spiritual values of charity and hospitality that had been planted in his soul as a child. He had little money, but even that was shared among his fellows if they had less—all part of the lifestyle of the Roncalli household back home.

During these years, Roncalli met Giacomo Maria Radini Tedeschi, who would later become bishop of Bergamo and whom Angelo would serve as personal secretary. Of all those who influenced his life by example, none would be more influential than his godfather, Zaverio, and his bishop, Monsignor Radini. Zaverio implanted within Angelo the great love of Jesus and trust in God's providence. And Radini showed Angelo, as a young priest, how to translate that into effective and helpful church governance.

Early Assignments

Angelo Roncalli was ordained a priest on 10 August 1904. His early assignments as a priest had a lasting influence on the man who would one day become pope.

Within a year of his ordination, Roncalli was appointed secretary to Bishop Radini. He also traveled around the entire continent of Europe and taught history at the local seminary. Bishop Radini and Angelo formed a great bond. Later in his life, Roncalli described Radini in this way:

> He was the polar star of my priesthood. His soul was more disposed to note merits than to exaggerate faults. He treated everybody with the greatest deference. He spoke with incomparable pleasantness, seasoning his conversation with unexpected witticisms. He was not authoritarian. He wanted all those around him to con-

tribute their energies to the apostolate and to assume their proper responsibilities. He was discreet. One remarked a depth of inexhaustible gaiety in his soul. (Fesquet, pp. 165–166)

Prior to being ordained, Roncalli served in the Italian army; he served later, as well, as a chaplain during the First World War. In his military service he found, as he seemed to find in everything, an opportunity to learn and to grow.

I am grateful for everything to the Lord, . . . but I especially thank Him for the fact that when I was twenty years old He willed that I should do my military service, and then, during the First World War, renew it as sergeant and chaplain. What a knowledge of the human soul one gains that way! What experience and what grace were given me to dedicate myself, to make sacrifices, to understand life and the apostolate of a priest. (Giovannetti, pp. 20–21)

In 1921 Roncalli was summoned to the Vatican by Pope Benedict XV to direct the Sacred Congregation for the Propagation of the Faith, which oversaw the finances of the Italian foreign missions. Benedict was a unique pontiff, more progressive and less fearful than others before and after him, and he gave Roncalli broad and sweeping authority to restructure this office and bring together the jealous national mission societies to make them more effective. Roncalli rose to the task, visiting all of Europe once again and succeeding in handling devout but proudly nationalistic churchmen. Significantly Roncalli did not savor this assignment at first, but he later wrote to the man who succeeded him as director: "I am convinced that if there were any good fruits of my work, that was because I took up this ministry out of pure obedience. Then the Lord gave me the grace to love it, and I left with sorrow" (Hebblethwaite, p. 107).

International Assignments

In 1925 Roncalli was named archbishop and was sent to Sofia, Bulgaria. Bulgaria had not had a papal representative for five centuries, and Roncalli was called on to balance the delicate relationships between anti-Roman local leadership and the Holy See. He was often frustrated during this period of his life, not understanding exactly what his mission in Bulgaria may have been. His lack of clarity about his role, however, did not decrease the vigor with which he approached his job. He began his work in Bulgaria by traveling to remote outposts to visit the few Catholics living there. The distinct differences between Catholic life in Bulgaria and in Rome were apparent in a letter he wrote in 1929:

> My heart breaks when I think that you in Rome can devise no further ways of making the triumph of Jesus in the Eucharist, carried in the arms of his Vicar, more spectacular, while here we don't even have oil to light the lamps in the chicken-coops we use as chapels. But these poor lamps are a beginning. (Hebblethwaite, p. 120)

Roncalli's strong and engaging personality was evident in his work in Bulgaria. Bulgarian Catholics knew him as *Diado*, which means "the good father." The attachment was mutual—twenty years later Roncalli still remembered Bulgaria fondly:

> I still keep a fine collection of photographs of these beautiful country places, and when I am tired I look through them again. Believe me, when I remember those dear people, my heart is moved and my eyes are full of tears. (Hebblethwaite, p. 120)

Istanbul was Roncalli's destination in 1935, when he was named Apostolic Delegate for Turkish and Greek Catholics. He learned the local languages and urged the people to use the vernacular rather than Latin in their liturgical ceremonies.

A liturgical movement opposed by Roman conservatives had started as far back as the previous century. It extolled the celebration of the Mass, along with the other sacraments, as essential to deepening the spiritual life of the faithful. It urged active and intelligent participation of the faithful in the rites themselves, something forbidden by the church since the sixteenth century because of its similarity to Protestant worship. This liturgical movement was strongly opposed by the members of the Roman Curia, yet Roncalli encouraged such participation on the part of the faithful under his care. His action provides a valuable clue to his own understanding of the church.

Roncalli interested himself in the entire Near East. His time in the Balkans and the Near East deepened within him a desire to unite the Eastern churches with Rome again. This desire followed him to the papacy.

Roncalli remained in Istanbul until after the Second World War ended. He was then appointed Papal Nuncio to France. There he charmed the entire nation, even its leader, the chilly Charles de Gaulle. In France Roncalli polished his abilities to bring together separated factions diplomatically and learned firsthand how to work amid cultural anticlericalism. He learned about the needs of the Catholic faithful in a new world in which political and spiritual lives had to be rebuilt in the wake of a devastating war. He witnessed the experimental worker-priest movement in France, was aware of the "new theology" brewing in that part of Europe, and personally involved himself in the question of whether the church in France, or indeed in all of modern Europe, would continue to decline or would experience a rebirth.

While in Paris Roncalli served as the Vatican's observer for the United Nations Educational, Scientific, and Cultural Organization (UNESCO). Roncalli's involvement with this worldwide cultural and educational movement gave him a strong sense of the church's place in the modern world.

In 1953 Roncalli was made a cardinal of the church, and he moved from France to Venice, as patriarch, in 1954. He told the people of Venice that at age seventy-four, he would finally be able to enjoy pastoral work, which had been his lifelong dream. Here too he polished his skills at administration, equipping himself to deal eventually with the many complex administrative problems at the Vatican, especially those associated with the calling of a council.

The Papacy

In October 1958 Pope Pius XII suffered a fatal stroke. In the conclave of the church's cardinals that followed Pius' funeral,

Cardinal Angelo Roncalli was elected, after eleven ballots, to be the new pope. When asked the ritual question by the dean of the cardinals, "By what name do you wish to be known?" Roncalli answered, "I will be called John." He explained:

> The name John is dear to me because it was the name of my father, because it is the dedication of the humble parish church where we were baptized, and because it is the name of innumerable cathedrals throughout the world. (Hebblethwaite, p. 286)

Most important, Roncalli chose the name John so that he could renew the instruction of the Apostle John. Said the new pope, "My children, love one another. Love one another because this is the greatest commandment of the Lord" (Hebblethwaite, p. 286).

Without hesitation or pause, Pope John XXIII brought charm, skill, and global vision to his work. Amazingly, by late that same year, he wondered aloud to his close confidant, Vatican Secretary of State Cardinal Tardini, what he could do to restore the lively faith of the early church and bring hope to modern times. Already, only a few months after his election, it had occurred to him that perhaps the answer would be a council.

On the feast of Saint Paul, 25 January 1959, Pope John celebrated a Mass for church unity. Eighteen cardinals were present for this feast. After the Mass the pope talked with them about the state of the church and his concerns for it. He announced his intention to hold a synod for the diocese of Rome with the purpose of reanimating the zeal and spirit of that local church, lodged as it was in the heart of the global Catholic church. Then, speaking about his hopes for the entire church, he announced that he had decided to revise canon law and to call an ecumenical council.

The response of these cardinals was not promising: they remained in dead silence. No one spoke even a single word in response. In the weeks and months that followed, John would learn about their silence. They could not, in their curial imaginations, believe that such a council was feasible, let alone desirable. They confronted him with objections, predictions of doom for the church, and their belief that it would be impossible to prepare for such an undertaking in less than ten or twenty years.

This stonewalling deepened the pope's determination to hold the council within the first years of his reign. To better understand Pope John's determination and his papacy, it is necessary to consider his view of the world, and the church, in which he lived.

Pope John's Worldview

Pope John was troubled by the state of the world in the late 1950s and wanted to clarify the church's role in it. He observed that while much of the world was in poverty, other parts of the world enjoyed unprecedented postwar plenty. All people lived under the increasing threat of nuclear war and had witnessed the power of the atom in Japan. The world was still stunned by the horrors of the Second World War and its unimaginable genocide. The unexpected success of totalitarianism and communism, and the increasing influence of atheism and materialism, caused alarm, confusion, and fear among many modern people.

Where was the Christian church in all this? Why did it remain so lacking in unity? Why were the men around him in the Vatican possessed of such parochial vision, and why were the bishops of the world not more vocal about the condition of the world?

Pope John knew that the hopes and dreams of men and women around the world were for peace and justice. And his own noble heart was filled with compassion for the world even while his personality naturally reached out to all around him. This combination of compassion and a gregarious personality may have been just the factors that needed to come together in a single man, a single pope, in order for a modern council of the Catholic church to be convened.

Care for the World

What is unique about Pope John's hopes for a council is that he was concerned about the condition of the world as much as he was about the condition of the church. His concern was, from the beginning, a pastoral one. There was no desire here to condemn any movement or persons in the world, no desire to clarify or state any new doctrines for the church. Such had been the business of previous councils. What Pope John wanted for this council, rather, was to reanimate the faith of Christians in order to allow them to contribute to the well-being of the world.

The council's own *Pastoral Constitution on the Church in the Modern World*, written after Pope John's death, echoed his desires when it said:

> In order to proceed here,
>> we must understand the world in which we live,
>>> its expectations,
>>> its longings,
>>>> and its often dramatic ways.
> In language understandable for each generation,
>> the Church should be able to give
>> a meaningful answer to questions people have
>>> about life:
>>> both now and after death.
> We must, in other words, read the signs of the times.
>
> (Huebsch, p. 128)

To Animate the World

Pope John's goal throughout his pontificate, to reanimate the faith of Christians, reflected the "natural religiosity" of his childhood in Sotto il Monte. How might Christian faith be reanimated? Certainly one place to begin was the point at which most Catholics come into closest contact with the institutional church itself: the rites of the Mass and the other sacraments, especially baptism. Pope John wanted to renew the sacramental life of the church, even to restore certain rites or practices of the early church. He sensed that sacramental life was the point at which renewal would get underway, that at that point the reanimation of the Christian spirit in the world would be launched.

The pope proclaimed his goal for the council by using a descriptive Italian word, *aggiornamento,* to indicate that he wanted to update the church's practices in many areas. Although conservative churchmen feared this and worked to be sure no major change actually occurred at Vatican II, most bishops and theologians understood this as a mandate to move forward, to undertake reforms begun so often before but thwarted by circumstance or politics.

The Early Communities

In considering the future of the church, Pope John took care not to ignore its past. Indeed, the early years of the church were marked by an energy and a spirit that made it possible for Christians to sustain even martyrdom for the sake of the faith. Baptism held a prominent place in the life of the community then, and was seen as a life-changing experience. Preparation for baptism often required many months or even years of learning the way of Jesus and growing into a commitment to the community of Christ. And because preparation for baptism was taken so seriously, early church members *lived* their faith, gathering often to share in the Lord's supper, taking heart from one another, sharing their material resources, trusting their conscience to guide them in moral decisions, and attracting others to the faith by their loving companionship.

Of course there had been politics among them then, too, but their gatherings were such that they rose above politics—or made holy use of them—for the sake of their faithful lives.

By the early 300s, however, the place of baptism in the life of the church had been greatly reduced by the actions of the emperor Constantine. For him the church was not so much a way to live the faith but a tool by which he could unite his realm and dominate the world. He lavished privilege on the clergy, built large churches, and demanded baptism for the masses of Europe. Using the early church councils, he and his successors pushed for doctrinal sameness in the church, providing them with a useful creed through which they could demand allegiance to the church, and hence to the realm. In most regards the church began to look like the imperial courts of the empire. It met in templelike buildings, its ministers wore imperial vestments, the rubrics of its rites became fixed, and its system of diocesan governance mimicked that of the empire. The deposit of faith was not lost, but the energy and spirit of the early centuries were.

Pope John longed to restore that lively faith of the first century. He himself talked publicly of a renewal for the church that would restore "the simple and pure lines that the face of the church of Jesus had at its birth." When asked at one point about his expectations of this council, Pope John moved toward the window and gestured as if to open it. He said, "The Council? I expect a little fresh air from it. . . . We must shake off the imperial dust that has accumulated on the throne of St. Peter since Constantine" (Fesquet, p. 157).

The Pope As Prophet

In this context Pope John was clearly a prophet who called the church back to its roots. He launched a new Pentecost within the church, a new epoch. "The idea of the Council," [he once said,] "did not ripen in me as the fruit of long meditation but came forth like the flower of an unexpected spring" (Fesquet, p. 156). Pope John's great opening speech at Vatican II provided a groundbreaking charter to the bishops of the world. It now stands in history alongside the speech of Stephen before his martyrdom and that of Peter on Pentecost, both in the Acts of the Apostles, as significant turning points in our church history.

Pope John lived to see only one session of the council, but he died with the same grace with which he had lived. Just a few days before his death, he summed up his life with these words:

> The secret of my ministry is in that crucifix you see opposite my bed. It's there so that I can see it in my first waking moment and before going to sleep. It's there, also, so that I can talk to it during the long evening hours. Look at

it. See it as I see it. Those open arms have been the pro-gramme of my pontificate: they say that Christ died for all, for all. No one is excluded from his love, from his for-giveness. (Hebblethwaite, p. 501)

Angelo Giuseppe Roncalli, the son of peasant farmers who became Pope John XXIII, died on the evening of 3 June 1963. During a session of the council several months later, Cardinal Suenens of Belgium, a close friend and confidant of Pope John, made a commemoration of him before the assembly. Here, in part, is what he said:

If one could reduce it all to a few words, I think one might say that John XXIII was a man singularly natural and su-pernatural at the same time. Nature and grace formed a single whole in a living unity full of charm and unfore-seen variety.

All sprang from the same source. He was entirely natural when supernatural, and was natural with such a supernatural spirit that it was impossible to detect the joining line. He breathed his faith, as he breathed physical and moral health, with open lungs. It has been written, "He lived in the presence of God with the simplicity of one who strolls along the streets of his native city." . . .

The natural, immediate, always thoughtful kindness of John XXIII was like the ray of sunlight that scatters the mist, dissolves the ice, and penetrates everywhere before we are aware of it, as if it had a perfect right to do so. A ray of light that creates optimism as it passes by gives joy with its sudden appearance, and is undaunted by any ob-stacle.

So John XXIII appeared to this world: not like the tropical sun which blinds people with the brilliance of its splendour, but like the humble familiar sun of every day, which is up there, in its appointed place, always true to it-self, even if sometimes momentarily veiled by a cloud, our own sun of which we take no notice because we are sure it is still there. (Balducci, pp. 67–68)

Praying with Pope John XXIII

Praying with Pope John will lead us inevitably to our own everyday lives. The secret in his spirituality was "commonness." Even as pope, that is what endeared him to people and what characterized his relationship with God. In the end it was a matter for Pope John of keeping perspective, a way of looking at others and the world and even himself, that emerged from faith. After all, he might have said that if God is truly the love that connects us, then we all stand on equal footing. Like the threads of a seamless garment, no strands are more noble or less noble than all the rest.

Humor

Humor is not often thought of as a first sign of the presence of God, but humor is inescapable in Pope John's life. He looked at himself, first and foremost, with a sense of self-deprecating humor, not out of a lack of confidence or self-esteem but in order to help him remain unpretentious. His approach to his adversaries was similar: always begin with a bit of humor. And likewise with friends, guests, colleagues, and even strangers—always be ready to observe the humorous side of the situation.

As we pray with Pope John, we gradually become aware ourselves of the humor that every situation seems to hold—when our perspective is larger than our own.

Charity

There was no greater virtue in Pope John's life than Christian charity. From his earliest journal entries to his deathbed, he cultivated this quality in himself. He recognized charity as the primary way we enter into the work of our ministry—not exactitude, not perfection, not authority, and not even orthodoxy. Charity for him was first.

Praying with him will likewise draw us into an examination in our own life of the primacy of charity among the virtues.

The Cross

No force was more powerful in Pope John's spirituality than the image of Christ, arms open wide to embrace the world, on the cross. John meditated on that image every day. Every evening before bedtime, he examined himself at the foot of that cross. There he found the wisdom that drove his own life: to open his own arms to all. By that he meant, literally, all. No one was excluded from the love of Christ as expressed by Pope John.

In praying with Pope John, we too are led to that same cross. We too learn to examine our attitudes and actions in the shadow of that image: Christ's arms open wide to embrace the world.

Trust in Divine Providence

Pope John had been reared and trained in the church that emerged from the Council of Trent in the sixteenth century. How did he dare to call an ecumenical council in the twentieth century in order to reform the church? Almost every one of his own Vatican officials opposed the council. How could he have proceeded with such singular vision? Opening the windows of the church to allow discussion would produce disagreement and radical ideas. How did he dare to allow this in a church ensconced in tradition? There can be only one answer: Pope John trusted in the Holy Spirit. He trusted that God is leading us to a new order of human relationships and to a new way of being present in today's world. John's trust in divine providence, rooted as it was in his deep faith, empowered him to go forward to places no one else may have gone.

In praying with Pope John, we will discover that the same faith is possible for us. We too can trust the "flashes of heavenly light" that illumine our life, and we too can take actions that change the world forever.

Saint John XXIII

I am not entirely sure what it takes these days for someone to enter the canon of the heavenly saints. But while writing this book, immersed in the life and work of Pope John, it often occurred to me that he himself was *present*, looking over my shoulder, urging me onward, noting the humor in this or that, reminding me that charity matters most of all, pointing out the cross that now hangs in my study, and teaching me to trust my intuitions as flashes of divine light.

He seems to *be here*, not absent.

I understand that it requires several proven miracles in order for someone to be canonized a saint. Just consider the influence of Vatican II on the world and on the church today: Hundreds of thousands of new lay ministers all around the world. People actually praying the Mass rather than merely attending it. Work for justice on a par with teaching about religion. Human dignity at the center of the church's witness. Warm and mutually beneficial relationships between Christians and Jews. Renewed trust in the human conscience. Harmony and dialog among the Christian denominations. And a new vigor in the Christian faith as we enter the next century.

Miracles, indeed!

✧ Meditation 1 ✧

Forgetting Oneself

Theme: We are all brothers and sisters. We all share one divine source of love. Once that is understood, position and protocol seem terribly unimportant.

Opening prayer:

O Brother Jesus,
>O Sister Spirit,
>O Divine Source of love,
>gather us now into one household of faith.
Teach us to humble ourselves
>so that the least among us is considered the most
>and the most, less.

About Pope John

During the papacy of John XXIII, it was decided that a bust of the pope should be cast as a lasting memorial to him. This is a common practice among key public figures, but Pope John turned this occasion, like all occasions he touched, into an opportunity for charity.

The sculptor chosen for the work was from Pope John's own home area of Bergamo in northern Italy. His name: Giacomo Manzù. This sculptor was not known to be a man of faith, and he would not have been the first choice of most members of the pope's staff. Pope John had been told before-hand about this man's opinions of the church and its clergy—opinions that tended toward the negative. Manzù lived a life quite outside "Catholic norms" in terms of his relationships, his politics (he was a communist), and his churchgoing.

Manzù was chosen nonetheless, and he and Pope John worked together to produce the bust. Pope John posed. Manzù sketched and molded clay. Meanwhile, their conversation was producing a lasting friendship.

After the first day of posing, Pope John sensed what the sculptor had been feeling: the need for them to know each other better. Pope John also may have been feeling the loneliness that seemed to come with the papacy, the feeling of being a "prisoner of the Vatican." In Manzù, Pope John saw someone who would not be too impressed with his position as pope, someone with whom he could relate on a more personal, ordinary level.

So, despite the carefully guarded privacy surrounding the pope's apartment in the Vatican, Pope John took Manzù there and gave him a remarkably complete tour of the place. At one point in the tour—which included the contents of the closets!—Pope John offered Manzù his own self, the "stuff" of his life, rather than his important position of pope. Manzù accepted, looking into the ordinary daily life of Pope John as a friend would do.

The tour included photos of Pope John's family, stories of his friends, mementos of previous assignments—the kind of things you would expect to find in anyone's apartment. Pope John and Giacomo Manzù demonstrated the essential first element that is required if people are to move from "official relationships" to real ones: they showed an interest in each other. They paid each other attention. And in the end both were richer.

Pause: Ask yourself, In what situations have I found myself tempted to pull rank, or to pretend to be more than I am, or to let my credentials give me power over others?

Pope John's Words

Slowly they had worked their way around the room, finally reaching the clothes closet which Pope John opened as though he was also curious to see inside. There were some white papal soutanes, a red shoulder cape, a cloak, and then—on a bottom shelf, two rows of papal slippers. They were red and white and on each one was sewn a golden cross. There was a pair of green ones, too, and all together it made a brilliant array. But it also seemed to leave the Pope uneasy.

"My shoes," he said, and looked at his visitor.

Manzù looked at the shoes and nodded.

"They don't fit as they should," he said.

Manzù nodded.

"They look sort of narrow."

"They are. The best shoes I ever had were in the Italian army. We Roncallis all have big feet and those were just right. You could walk in them for miles and miles and hardly feel it."

"These must be hard to walk in."

"Terrible," he said. "But I think it's part of the conspiracy here to prevent me from walking out of the Vatican. Every time I go outside, they get excited as though Italy was too dangerous for a Pope." (Pepper, p. 60)

Reflection

Pope John's spirituality emerged from that period of Catholic piety in which it was taught that denying oneself, even in the extreme, was an acceptable end in itself. It involved a forgetting of oneself, although not in the unhealthy sense of foregoing the necessities of life, such as nutrition, companionship, or a household. In this spirituality forgetting oneself meant forgetting one's position. If one is pope, one should forget about that and just be human. If one is poor, one also should forget about that and just be human. It is our humanness that connects us, as Pope John showed Manzù. A tour of one's closets is very private and revealing for anyone, but Pope

John never saw himself as pope first. He saw himself first as a brother, a brother to all those near him. And as a brother, the first rule is not protocol but charity.

What happened between Pope John and Manzù was not that Pope John condescended to speak to Manzù and share his personal life with him. Nor did Pope John have an "agenda" to carry out by relating to this nonreligious communist. What happened was a mutual sharing, a give and take. Pope John and Manzù became friends with each other.

There is a huge lesson in this. Moving toward one another in mutual charity and love is more important than any other "work" we do as Christians. It is the first law. The way to the heart of the Lord, someone has said, is never traveled alone. It isn't how much work we accomplish that matters. It isn't how firmly we hold the reins of our positions. It isn't how many people are in our churches. And it isn't in how much we command the respect of others through our offices in the church or society. In the end, as Pope John knew so well, it is through friendship and love that we move closer to the heart of Jesus.

✧ Examine your own personal and professional life for those situations where true friendship is possible.

✧ In your meditation time, consider how you prioritize your values. What is most important: your position? your influence? your command of the situation? demanding that others respect you? following the law? friendship? charity? lasting love?

✧ Consider who within your circle of acquaintances and coworkers is asking for attention from you. What prevents you from offering it to him or her?

✧ Give someone a tour of your personal living space. What stories would you tell them? What details of your life would you include? How would you reveal your true self in such a tour?

God's Word

God has appointed in the church first apostles, second prophets, third teachers; then deeds of power, then gifts of healing, forms of assistance, forms of leadership, various kinds of tongues. Are all apostles? Are all prophets? Are all teachers? Do all work miracles? Do all possess gifts of healing? Do all speak in tongues? Do all interpret? But strive for the greater gifts. And I will show you a still more excellent way.

If I speak in the tongues of mortals and of angels, but do not have love, I am a noisy gong or a clanging cymbal. And if I have prophetic powers, and understand all mysteries and all knowledge, and if I have all faith, so as to remove mountains, but do not have love, I am nothing. If I give away all my possessions, and if I hand over my body so that I may boast, but do not have love, I gain nothing. (1 Corinthians 12:28—13:3)

Closing prayer:

O Divine Friend and Companion,
    teach us your ways,
    the ways of love.
Help us put aside the competition that divides us,
    the arrogance that isolates us,
    the silence that keeps us private,
    and the domineering attitudes that
        place us over and against one another.
Develop within us a spirit of charity,
    and the humility that makes us accessible
        to one another,
        no matter our position or rank.
Give us the joy that comes from friendship. Amen.

Charity Above All Else

Theme: Christian charity toward all men and women grows out of our spirituality and our deep personal conviction that in the end we will be judged on how well we have loved—and nothing else.

Opening prayer:

O Divine Source of charity and love,
    grant us the humility to choose love
    even in the face of rejection and hatred.
Shape our hearts and minds
    to more closely reflect Jesus,
    and guide our souls
    into your way. Amen.

About Pope John

On 26 December 1958, Pope John did something that astonished members of his own staff as well as the people of Rome—he visited the inmates in a local prison.

As he entered the high, gloomy rotunda from which the corridors to the triple-tiered cell blocks radiated, he was touched by the sight of an exquisite crêche made by the inmates. A thousand prisoners in loose, flapping, convict-striped uniforms were assembled there to greet him. Pope John addressed them as, "Dear Sons and Brothers," and told them that his own brother had once been arrested for hunting without a license, and that he understood how a man may break the law to steal for his hungry family. "In your first letter home," he said, "say that the Pope came to see you, that he was here among you. And in my Holy Mass and in my daily breviary I will have a special thought and intense affection for each of you and for all your dear ones."

The prisoners knew he meant it. They felt the strong current of his love and the dynamic power of his sheer goodness flowing into them, as they stood together singing *Adeste Fidelis*. The officials, unduly nervous as officials always are, had mapped out a course for the Pope's inspection tour marked by a red carpet. He soon veered off it, meandering down the dank and musty corridors while the prisoners knelt to kiss his ring. One old man with a long police record asked humbly if the Pope's message of hope was also for him. "I have made many mistakes, Holy Father," he said.

Bending over the kneeling man, John wiped his tears away; then he raised him and embraced him with a great bear-hug saying, "I looked into your eyes with my eyes. I have put my heart near your heart."

When the Pope came to the cell block where the incorrigibles were confined he saw the grated doors placed there to keep them in. In his most commanding voice he ordered, "Open the gates. Do not bar them from me. They are all children of our Lord." (Hatch, pp. 217–218)

Pause: Have you ever placed yourself at risk, on the line, in the name of charity? Under what circumstances can you imagine doing so?

Pope John's Words

One of the similes used by St. Francis de Sales, which I love to repeat, is: "I am like a bird singing in a thicket of thorns"; this must be a continual inspiration to me. So, I must say very little to anyone about the things that hurt me. Great discretion and forbearance in my judgments of men and situations: willingness to pray particularly for those who may cause me suffering, and in everything great kindness and endless patience, remembering that any other sentiment or mixture of sentiments, *à la Macédoine,* as they say here, is contrary to the spirit of the Gospel and of evangelic perfection. So long as charity may triumph, at all costs, I would choose to be considered as of little worth. (*Journal of a Soul,* p. 218)

Reflection

The Christian life, when formed and developed in the fashion of Jesus, is full of simple, small decisions. Every hour of every day we choose how to live. Oh, the commitment to Christ is made all in a moment at baptism, to be sure. But the living out of that commitment develops all day long.

It is necessary for us to be on the lookout constantly for ways we can show love to one another—almost as if we were in competition with one another over who can be the most loving. Throughout our days together as families and friends, we can find these moments, from our morning rising to our evenings: in small but important ways, we seek to please one another, to surprise one another with affection. It isn't the big gifts in life that sustain us but the daily bread of a shared and loving life.

In our encounters throughout the day at work, at school, in our parish, in volunteer positions, in commerce—wherever we are and whatever we do—we can put charity first. We can make or take the time to visit those who are lonely, sick, or in prison. We can recycle to help the earth. We can reuse materials to reduce our cost of living so we will have more to share with those who are in need. We can work for peace, eliminate gossip, support outsiders, welcome strangers, and generally establish love as the guide for our lives.

And most important, we can *pay attention* to those who are closest to us, those we see every day. We can offer them attention and affection without embarrassment or fail.

Each of the following is a moment in which charity is a choice. We make many other choices, too.

✦ We choose between a kind word, even when we are tired or feeling used, and a harsh word.

✦ We choose between negative judgments of one another and judgments that leave room for the possibility of error on our part.

✦ We choose between going the extra mile, even at the end of a busy day, or turning into ourselves in self-pity.

✦ We choose between stopping on the way home to pick up that simple little gift for someone we love or driving straight through.

✦ We choose between a charitable silence or the tendency to comment unkindly toward others' behavior.

It is always a choice, and that is the insight Pope John brought to the spiritual journey. Like him we must develop this charity as a value—a primary value—by examining our everyday activities and decisions.

One way to do this is through a sort of evening reflection on what has passed that day, a modern sort of "examination of conscience." Not with an eye to what laws or rules we may have broken but with an eye to how thoroughly and insistently we have loved, with an eye to how much on the lookout we have been for ways we can offer one another charity.

✧ It is helpful in the Christian journey to pay attention to the small things, the details of life. In this way we will find the key to spiritual growth. What are the small ways in your everyday life in which you can humbly offer charity to others?

✧ Engage in an examination of conscience at the end of each day.

✧ There is a difference between genuine charity and manipulative giving. In the former the welfare of those receiving charity is what is important. In the latter the giver of the charity tries to gain control through generosity. Consider this in your own life. Where do you draw the line?

✧ Make a list of people—individuals or groups—you find it most difficult to treat with charity: those you resent, dislike, or compete with; those who have done something to hurt you or a loved one; those who seem selfish, entitled, or lazy. How could you find opportunities to offer them charity? What would you lose if you did? What would you gain?

✧ Who in your neighborhood or town is most in need of genuine love and charity? Those in jails? Those with AIDS? Those who are homeless? Those who are wealthy? Those in the arts? Those who are young? Plan ways to reach them with your charity this month.

God's Word

Let love be genuine; hate what is evil, hold fast to what is good; love one another with mutual affection; outdo one another in showing honor. Do not lag in zeal, be ardent in spirit, serve the Lord. Rejoice in hope, be patient in suffering, persevere in prayer. Contribute to the needs of the saints; extend hospitality to strangers.

Bless those who persecute you; bless and do not curse them. Rejoice with those who rejoice, weep with those who weep. Live in harmony with one another; do not be haughty, but associate with the lowly; do not claim to be wiser than you are. Do not repay anyone evil for evil, but take thought for what is noble in the sight of all. If it is possible, so far as it depends on you, live peaceably with all. (Romans 12:9–18)

Closing prayer:

We call on you, O God of love,
    and recognize that you are with us
    in all we say and do.
Now grant that we might be earnest in our pursuit of love
    so that we might turn moments of darkness
    into moments of light.
Guide us to live in such a way
    that all will see in us
    a humble charity that reveals through us
    your presence to the world. Amen.

✧ **Meditation 3** ✧

Do Not Eat Alone

Theme: Companionship at the table is a great Christian value, one that modern life seems to militate against.

Opening prayer:

O Jesus, guest and convener of meals,
    grant us the grace of good dining!
Join us, we pray, at our tables
    as we join one another
    in our meals of healing,
        hospitality,
        daily sustenance,
        and celebration.
Grant us peace in our meals,
    joy in our companionship with one another,
        and gratitude for all you have given us. Amen.

About Pope John

Not long after being elected to the papacy, Pope John took up residence in the papal apartments. These private apartments are hidden well inside Vatican City. John felt a little like a prisoner there, unable to come and go as he pleased and, more important to him, unable to invite friends to daily meals. It had become a custom for the pope to dine alone.

Pope John confided to his secretary, [Monsignor Loris] Capovilla, that he was unable to sleep through the night any more. He felt lonely, and this kept him awake. He needed more conversation and more social stimulation to help him lose this feeling of being deserted. . . .

[Pope John] simply could not accustom himself to the habit of eating all by himself, a practice which Pius XII had always maintained. In a very short time Capovilla was invited to join him at the table. The Pope's appetite improved immediately. Shortly afterwards he invited the cardinals of the Curia to be his table companions, one after the other. Little by little, bishops from all over the world, when they made their *ad limina* visits to Rome, were invited to join him for lunch or dinner. (Klinger, p. 29)

Pope John had done it. He had broken the custom of dining alone—and he would never return to it!

Pause: Ask yourself: With whom have I recently shared meals? Did they offer me the companionship that Pope John recognized he needed? Did I offer them the same?

Pope John's Words

Once a distinguished luncheon companion ventured to remind John of the solitary eating habits of Pius XII. "Well and good," John replied. "I value tradition and I grant that my predecessors did, too. I must confess, however, that I have never found any place in the Bible which suggests that the Pope should eat alone." (Klinger, p. 29)

Reflection

With whom do *you* eat? In modern society many people eat alone; many eat standing up at the kitchen sink, or with one hand on the steering wheel of their moving car. For many the meal is an inconvenience. It would be better if we didn't have to eat; it just gets in the way of more important things: working, generating income, being busy, watching television.

This decline in shared dining has been accelerating in recent years, and many people have simply given up on ever recovering shared meals. Even the grocery industry has recognized this, filling its freezer cases with individual-serving sizes of most prepared foods. In many situations, such as in fast-food restaurants, large numbers of people eat "alone together." It isn't so much a shared meal as a shared eating space.

Unfortunately those on the Christian journey, including church workers and volunteers, are often among the worst offenders. "I don't have time to eat, I have to get to a meeting." Or, "I'll just run out and get something quick from Burger World."

It doesn't take a very thorough review of the Gospels to realize how important shared meals and parties are for those who are serious about the spiritual journey. Jesus did a lot of his work in the context of meals. He taught Simon the Pharisee a thing or two while sitting at Simon's dinner table. He fed five thousand hungry people with just a few fishes and loaves of bread. And nearly every appearance of the Risen Lord occurred in the context of a meal: at Emmaus in the blessing and breaking of the bread; in the upper room, where Christ says "Give me to eat"; and in that famous fish fry on the beach in the last chapter of the Gospel of John.

And of course the most lasting and profound remembrance we have of Jesus is a meal—the Eucharist.

The word *companion* comes from Latin sources meaning "those with whom we break bread." Those with whom we eat. The women, men, and children with whom Jesus ate: these were the ones with whom he shared his last meal. It must have been an intimate and wonderful party!

So let's get serious about making the meal more central in our Christian journey. The textbook for small Christian communities, families, religious communities, and other households should be *The Joy of Cooking*. Here is found the recipe for growth and shared life. Cooking, dining, cleaning up, and then later, remembering the meal—these are what drive daily life in Christ. These are the bread and butter of life.

This is the way Christians can lay claim once again to Sabbath, which has been given over to commercialism in much of the world. Here is a way to attract our children and youth to be part of a religious conversation in our homes. This is the organizing method for parishes: Eat together. Nothing else is needed—no discussion guides, no programs, no agenda—just the meal, shared and lasting. If you cook it, they will come.

✧ Buy a cookbook and invite people to dinner. Think about your guest list: does it include people who are marginalized in your community?

✧ Organize a way for your faith community to start sharing meals on a regular basis, and include in that a way for the "uninvited" to be received.

✧ Sit down and think about how your life is organized. Where do meals fit in? Are they a nuisance, a necessary burden? Or are they an opportunity for companionship?

✧ Commit yourself to cooking and baking again: fill your home with the activity, aroma, and enterprise of caring for yourself and your loved ones. Pull out those pots and pans. Dig through the drawers for those old favorite family recipes. Start slowly, with one meal a week. But plan to increase it to two or three—or finally, every day!

God's Word

After these things Jesus showed himself again to the disciples by the Sea of Tiberias; and he showed himself in this way. Gathered there together were Simon Peter, Thomas called the Twin, Nathanael of Cana in Galilee, the sons of Zebedee, and two others of his disciples. Simon Peter said to them, "I am going fishing." They said to him, "We will go with you." They went out and got into the boat, but that night they caught nothing.

Just after daybreak, Jesus stood on the beach; but the disciples did not know that it was Jesus. Jesus said to them, "Children, you have no fish, have you?" They answered him, "No." He said to them, "Cast the net to the right side of the boat, and you will find some." So they cast it, and now they were not able to haul it in because there were so many fish. That disciple whom Jesus loved said to Peter, "It is the Lord!" When Simon Peter heard that it was the Lord, he put on some clothes, for he was naked, and jumped into the sea. But the other disciples came in the boat, dragging the net full of fish, for they were not far from the land, only about a hundred yards off.

When they had gone ashore, they saw a charcoal fire there, with fish on it, and bread. Jesus said to them, "Bring some of the fish that you have just caught." So Simon Peter went aboard and hauled the net ashore, full of large fish, a hundred fifty-three of them; and though there were so many, the net was not torn. Jesus said to them, "Come and have breakfast." Now none of the disciples dared to ask him, "Who are you?" because they knew it was the Lord. Jesus came and took the bread and gave it to them, and did the same with the fish. This was now the third time that Jesus appeared to the disciples after he was raised from the dead.

When they had finished breakfast, Jesus said to Simon Peter, "Simon son of John, do you love me more than these?" He said to him, "Yes, Lord; you know that I love you." Jesus said to him, "Feed my lambs." A second time he said to him, "Simon son of John, do you love me?" He said to him, "Yes, Lord; you know that I love you." Jesus said to him, "Tend my sheep." He said to him the third time, "Simon son of John, do you love me?" Peter felt hurt because he said to him the third time, "Do you love me?" And he said to him, "Lord, you know everything; you know that I love you." Jesus said to him, "Feed my sheep." (John 21:1–17)

Closing prayer:

O Great Provider of everything good,
    come to us now
    as we sit down to dine together.
Join us at this table.
    Fill our hearts with gratitude for these gifts
    and fill our conversation with charity
    toward one another.
May our bodies be nourished by this food
    and our souls filled with the great comfort
    of being with one another. Amen.

✧ **Meditation 4** ✧

Seek Peace and Follow After It

Theme: It is the duty of the Christian to seek peace on all fronts—peace of heart, social peace, and international peace—because Jesus Christ, around whom we unite, is the Prince of Peace.

Opening prayer:

O Jesus, our great and loving peacemaker,
    guide our own hearts now to live in peace.
Let your will for us,
    lived in love and joy,
    be the basis of that peace.
May our hearts be so moved by the love
      you have shown us
    that we now turn in love toward one another,
    a love that drives us to seek peace. Amen.

About Pope John

To say that the promotion of peace—peace within men and women, social peace, and international peace—was important to Pope John is to understate their priority in his papacy. He turned to this theme repeatedly in both public and private decisions and remarks.

For example, on 12 October 1962, the day after the opening of Vatican II, Pope John addressed diplomats from seventy-nine nations who had sent one kind of delegate or another to the Vatican for the events. Vatican II would be a religious event, he told them, but he also hoped it would contribute to the development of world peace. This peace, he said, should be "based on growing respect for the human person and so leading to freedom of religion and worship" (Hebblethwaite, p. 435). Among the diplomats in the room was G. Frederick Reinhardt, from the United States, who perhaps knew that within a week the Cuban missile crisis would bring the world to the edge of war.

In the midst of that crisis, Pope John conceived the idea to write an encyclical on war and peace. Just a short time later though, Pope John learned from his doctors that he had a serious case of cancer, and that he had less than a year to live. Remarkably, John became more determined than ever to write the encyclical. He seems to have decided that although he would not live to see the end of the Council, he could at least complete work on this important document.

Despite his serious and painful illness, Pope John's passion to complete this message to the world did not wane. He saw it as a way to extend the love of Christ to the world, and he was committed to extending Christ's love in this way.

The following spring, Cardinal Suenens of Belgium represented Pope John in New York City at the United Nations. He presented to the world body the official copy of this papal document, which had been given the title *Pacem in Terris*, or *Peace on Earth*. *Pacem in Terris* was addressed to all the people of the world, not merely to Catholics, which broke from the usual practice for encyclicals. *Pacem in Terris*, Suenens told the assembly, may be called a symphony for peace, like Beethoven's Ninth. Its theme is peace, he told them, which needs truth as its foundation, justice as its norm, love as its driving force, and freedom as its setting.

While few such major papal pronouncements are written personally by the pope himself, this one seems to reflect very closely the views of Pope John XXIII. And much of its spirit found its way into core documents of Vatican II, published as it was between the first and second sessions of the Council.

Pause: How central to your faith is peacemaking? How do you express it as a priority in your daily life? Do you act for peace yourself, or do you leave it to others?

Pope John's Words

In the world of today, how many roads to peace have been proposed and imposed? . . .

But human efforts in the matter of universal peace-making are still far from the point where heaven and earth meet.

The fact is that true peace cannot come save from God. It has only one name: the peace of Christ. It has one aspect, that impressed on it by Christ who, as if to anticipate the counterfeits of man, emphasized: "Peace I leave with you, my peace I give to you."

The appearance of true peace is threefold:

Peace of heart: peace is before all else an interior thing, belonging to the spirit, and its fundamental condition is a loving and filial dependence on the will of God. "Thou hast made us for Thyself, O Lord, and our heart is restless till it rests in Thee."

All that weakens, that breaks, that destroys this conformity and union of wills is opposed to peace. . . .

Social peace: this is solidly based on mutual and reciprocal respect for the personal dignity of man. The Son of God was made man, and His redeeming act concerns not only mankind as a whole but also the individual man.

He "loved me and gave himself up for me." Thus spoke St. Paul to the Galatians. And if God has loved man to such a degree, that indicates that we belong to Him and that the human person has an absolute right to be respected. . . .

The disturbances which unsettle the internal peace of nations trace their origins chiefly to this source: that man has been treated almost exclusively as a machine, a piece of merchandise, a worthless cog in some great machine or a mere productive unit. . . .

International peace: the basis of international peace is, above all, truth. For in international relations, too, the Christian saying is valid: "The truth shall make you free."

It is necessary, then, to overcome certain erroneous ideas: the myths of force, of nationalism, or of other things that have poisoned fraternal life among peoples. . . .

Along with and enlightened by truth, should come justice. This removes the causes of quarrels and wars, solves the disputes, fixes the tasks, defines the duties and gives the answer to the claims of each party.

Justice in its turn must be integrated and sustained by Christian charity. (*The Encyclicals*, pp. 202–204)

Reflection

A heady period of Christian history occurred immediately after the conclusion of the Second Vatican Council, when Christians worldwide became active workers for peace. The peace movement, as it was called, seemed to be everyone's business. Participants made a strong connection between peace and faith, beginning with the premise that working for peace was a demand of faith.

Alongside the movement for world peace came another movement, one with equal force, for justice within nations and among the peoples of the world. Fueled by the insight that real peace is the result of having established justice, along with the theological movements emerging in the Third World, many Christians began to understand that this work was not optional for Christians but constitutive of the Christian life. In other words one could not be a Christian and ignore the work for peace and justice.

But in the decades since the Council ended, this focus on working for peace and justice has diminished for many Christians. Once again Christians seem ready to accept the development of armaments and the manufacture of the apparatus of war as acceptable and necessary.

What happened? Did world leaders, seeing Christians unite with other peace-loving people to demand an end to war, take their warmaking into secret? Did commercial firms involved in the making of armaments hire public relations firms to make their industry more palatable to us? Did war and the threat of war come to a miraculous end? Has justice been established on Earth?

In the midst of a busy, modern Christian life, it is very easy to compromise priorities and forget that Jesus is the Prince of Peace. What does this mean? Pope John, living as he did during the critical period of the early sixties, remembered well the bombing of Japan, the destruction from World War II in Europe, and the threat that international tensions posed to the world. We are further away from those events now, but if we read the morning newspaper next to the Gospels, we can still see that violence threatens the world.

What Pope John taught about peace still applies, and the call to work as peacemakers is still clear. The problems are still with us:

✦ Men and women today are treated as units of commerce, disposed of as easily as too much freight in the warehouse.

✦ Ethnic groups continue to hate one another and often attack one another.

✦ Families are still exposed to terrible violence on television, from talk-show fights to homicide to reckless treatment of others.

✦ Modern comedy seems based on mockery and cynicism.

✦ Individuals continue to live with fear, anger, and aggression.

✦ Nations still posture against one another, and the arms race is still going strong.

✦ Poverty still threatens much of the world.

✦ Women, men, and children continue to live in dangerous situations.

✦ We fear and hate one another.

✦ We are still cut apart by greed and competition.

Will the world sink into darkness, or will it emerge into a new renaissance of peace? The answer to this question is in the hands of Christians and all men and women of good will.

✧ In your life where do you most feel the lack of peace? What inner conflicts most need healing and reconciliation? With what feeling, pain, or memory have you failed to deal?

✧ In your home what are the causes of pain and conflict? How can you introduce love where there is hatred or enmity at home?

✧ In your community or parish, where are the conflicts? How can they be resolved in such a way that others can see in you an abundant expression of the love of Jesus Christ? What groups are most excluded? What people are most mocked? What can you do to stem this?

✧ In your nation what conflict seems most likely to emerge into full-scale violence? Who is hated, and against whom are hate crimes committed? Where is misunderstanding most prevalent? How can you join forces with others to bring an end to fear, hatred, and aggression against others?

✧ In your world what imbalance of justice makes war most likely? What movement for peace can you join? How can you help turn your church community into a peace movement?

✧ Study the encyclical *Pacem in Terris* and develop the principles for a Christian peace movement for today's world.

God's Word

Then his father Zechariah was filled with the Holy Spirit and spoke this prophecy:
"Blessed be the Lord God of Israel,
for he has looked favorably on his people and
redeemed them.
He has raised up a mighty savior for us
in the house of his servant David,
as he spoke through the mouth of his holy prophets
from of old,

that we would be saved from our enemies and
from the hand of all who hate us.
Thus he has shown the mercy promised to our
ancestors,
and has remembered his holy covenant,
the oath that he swore to our ancestor Abraham,
to grant us that we, being rescued from the
hands of our enemies,
might serve him without fear, in holiness and
righteousness
before him all our days.
And you, child, will be called the prophet of the Most
High;
for you will go before the Lord to prepare his
ways,
to give knowledge of salvation to his people
by the forgiveness of their sins.
By the tender mercy of our God,
the dawn from on high will break upon us,
to give light to those who sit in darkness and in the
shadow of death,
to guide our feet into the way of peace."
(Luke 1:67–79)

Closing prayer:

O Mary, queen of peace
pray for us
that we might have the will to follow your Son
on the road to peace.
Implant within us personal peace
through constant reconciliation of what troubles us.
Develop among us peace as sisters and brothers,
sharing one community,
one parish,
one family.
And lead us to active pursuit of peace within our nation
and among the nations of the world. Amen.

✧ **Meditation 5** ✧

An Ecumenical Spirit

Theme: Christian unity is not an optional, political position within the church but an essential goal for all Christians. It is central because such unity isn't merely a matter of what humans want but of what Christ most wants for the church.

Opening prayer:

Jesus, source of our unity and peace,
    we pray now for the grace of ecumenism.
Give us the humility to see others' truths,
    the courage to embrace them openly,
    and the desire to be one,
        as you taught us by your life. Amen.

About Pope John

The key shift introduced by Pope John in the discussion of Christian unity was a new language, a language focused on love rather than on legal reunification. This marked a significant change in attitude and, in the end, pervaded the Second Vatican Council's discussions of unity. In part this emerged from Pope John's own generous attitude toward the world and those around him. In part, too, it emerged from his faith, for he firmly believed that Christian unity was not an optional dimension of his program, not an agenda item for the

Council, but the chief vocation of his pontificate. He firmly believed that there would be one flock and one shepherd, not out of human desire but because Jesus Christ wishes it to be so. Who are we, he asked, to argue with that?

Knowing the propensity of his colleagues in the Vatican to argue the fine points of any theological position based on scholastic scholarship or the teachings of popes over the centuries, Pope John studiously avoided any description of unity that contained in it a theological position. He used a rich blend of analogies with language drawn largely from the Gospels, not so much to initiate politico-ecclesiastic activity as to encourage love.

Time magazine correspondent Robert Blair Kaiser once described Pope John as "less a theologian than an intuitive thinker," and described the Pope's approach to ecumenism as a "general theology of encounter, a movement of the Church into the world as it is." Kaiser related a brief story that took place when the future pope was nuncio to France:

> "Why can't we come together?" Archbishop Roncalli was supposed to have asked a Protestant in Paris. Said the Protestant: "There are different ideas . . .
>
> "Ideas, ideas," answered Roncalli with a shrug, "Ideas are such little things among friends." (Kaiser, p. 31)

Pause: Ask yourself: In what ways do I remain "triumphal" about my own Christian sect? What doors must I open in order to allow the grace of ecumenism to flourish among us?

Pope John's Words

> The vexing problem of the broken unity of the heritage of Christ still remains; obstacles still hinder its solution; it portends a long road of serious difficulties and uncertainties. . . .
>
>   . . . We intend to pursue humbly but fervently the duty urged upon Us by the words and example of Jesus,

the divine Good Shepherd, which He continues to speak to Us as he views the harvests which whiten the vast missionary fields: "Them also I must bring . . . and there shall be one fold and one shepherd"; and which He speaks to Us in the prayer raised to His Father in His last hours on earth, when the supreme sacrifice was imminent: "That all may be one, even as thou, Father, in me and I in thee; that they also may be one in us that the world may believe that thou hast sent me." (*The Encyclicals*, p. 139)

Reflection

In the spiritual life, we are pilgrims, but we move forward with one another: those we love most tenderly first, those others in our near circles, but also all those who share our faith and believe with us in the power of the grace of Jesus Christ. For most Christians today, as for those over the past four centuries, we consider "all those who share our faith" to be those who share our religious politics, those who are members of our particular Christian sect.

But doesn't this fall short of the imagination of Jesus? Didn't he dream of a unity far greater than this? Pope John believed that if we cannot come to agreement on each fine point of our doctrinal language and beliefs, we can at least allow the fire of charity to dominate in our relations to one another. He believed the fire of charity would lead us on the path to unity.

This suggests that the Christian journey should not be seen merely as a journey to the heart of our church magisterium and legal system, but truly as a journey to the heart of Jesus, a heart of love.

And it also suggests we should allow this to translate not merely into tolerance for one another but into active love. It leads us to seek one another out. It leads us to invite one another to friendship, dialog, and prayer. And, as the Vatican II document on ecumenism suggests, in order for the grace of ecumenism to be present, it must lead us to eucharistic sharing whenever appropriate. And all this not out of human desire but because it is the desire of Christ for us.

What a challenge to our spiritual journeys! How profound and mysterious this is. In Pope John's final prayers for the church, as in Jesus' final prayers, this goal was uppermost. *Ut unum sint*—that all may be one.

What is uppermost for us? Is it the doctrinal purity and completeness of our own denomination? Is it a carefully defined and exclusive guest list at our liturgies? Are we scandalized by the suggestion that the power of love may compel us to open our arms to embrace one another, regardless of denomination?

Often our divisions don't come down to core beliefs, such as those surrounding Jesus, the Spirit, or even prayer and the Scriptures. They are based on how our particular church organizes its own inner life, its "discipline." Such matters as who is ordained to ministerial roles, who is invited to receive Communion, who is welcome to marry, or how community decisions are reached often dominate our differences. Christian churches differ widely in these matters, as well as in others. It is here that we often break off dialog and begin to hurl hateful slogans at one another. Here is the point where loving one another becomes a formidable challenge for us.

The key is this: We should not allow distinctions of language or discipline—all matters decided by humans—to divide us from the core of the Gospel. To do so seems to blaspheme the Holy Spirit promised by Christ to us. It seems to work against the central goals of Christ's own mission that all might be one, *ut unum sint*.

✧ Make a list of the obstacles that prevent us from seeking Christian unity with the fervor of Pope John and Jesus Christ. Go back through the list and consider how you would explain your list to Christ and the Apostles.

✧ If you were drawing up a guest list for a dinner party in your home, what would be the criteria you would use to develop the list? Would religious denomination, doctrinal purity, or profession of faith be among them?

✧ Invite those with whom you disagree most to join you at table in a dialog about your distinct beliefs. Examine the basis of these beliefs and find ways not necessarily to agree but to love one another beyond your disagreements.

✧ In your parish or faith community, organize dialog for those many families who live in ecumenical households these days. What special hospitality is offered to spouses and family members? How are children trained when more than one religious tradition is observed in the home? What experiments might you conceive to help support the spiritual lives of these families more fully?

God's Word

All mine are yours, and yours are mine; and I have been glorified in them. And now I am no longer in the world, but they are in the world, and I am coming to you. Holy Father, protect them in your name that you have given me, so that they may be one, as we are one. While I was with them, I protected them in your name that you have given me. I guarded them, and not one of them was lost except the one destined to be lost, so that the scripture might be fulfilled. But now I am coming to you, and I speak these things in the world so that they may have my joy made complete in themselves. I have given them your word, and the world has hated them because they do not belong to the world, just as I do not belong to the world. I am not asking you to take them out of the world, but I ask you to protect them from the evil one. They do not belong to the world, just as I do not belong to the world. Sanctify them in the truth; your word is truth. As you have sent me into the world, so I have sent them into the world. And for their sakes I sanctify myself, so that they also may be sanctified in truth.

I ask not only on behalf of these, but also on behalf of those who will believe in me through their word, that they may all be one. As you, Father, are in me and I am in you, may they also be in us, so that the world may believe that you have sent me. The glory that you have given me I have given them, so that they may be one, as we are one,

I in them and you in me, that they may become complete-
ly one, so that the world may know that you have sent me
and have loved them even as you have loved me. (John
17:10–23)

Closing prayer:

O Great Spirit of unity,
    we come before you in humility
    because our hardheartedness and pride prevent us
        from seeing your love among us.
Take away from us all selfish desires
    and fill us only with the desire for you.
In you we will live and have our being
    and in you we will seek one another's welfare
    and work for one another's benefit.
Grant us the grace of an ecumenical spirit
    and give us the wisdom to recognize ways
    to organize ourselves so that
        we become a reflection of you
        to the world in which we live. Amen.

More Than Merely Christian

Theme: Christians are called to serve all human beings, not merely Christians, and to an expanded vision of what it means to be part of God's family.

Opening prayer:

O Great Founder of the human family,
 teach us to love one another as sisters and brothers
 living in your divine energy.
Grant us the grace to open ourselves
 to a new understanding
 of your mercy and love. Amen.

About Pope John

Before he was elected to the papacy, Pope John served in several key positions in the church. He served the churches of Bulgaria, Turkey, Greece, France, and Venice, Italy, before his final move to Rome in 1958. During this time he developed an attitude and language of openness toward non-Catholics. He saw all men and women as his concern and never failed to be gently inclusive in his address to the people.

This feature of his life contributed greatly to the spirit he brought to the papacy and especially to Vatican II. There the bishops of the world drew from his spirit a sense of concern for the entire human family. In fact the first official statement of the council was addressed not to Catholics but to all members of the human family.

In his farewell remarks to the Bulgarian people in November 1934, Angelo Roncalli said:

> According to a tradition still preserved in Catholic Ireland, on Christmas Eve every house sets a light in the window, in order to let Joseph and Mary know, in case they are passing by that night, looking for shelter, that inside there is a family, awaiting them around the fire and around the table laden with the gifts of God. . . . No one knows the ways of the future! Wherever I might go in the world, if someone from Bulgaria should pass by my house, at night, in distress, he will find a lamp lit in my window. Knock! Knock! I will not ask you if you are a Catholic or not; it is enough that you are my brother from Bulgaria: enter! Two brotherly arms will embrace you, the warm heart of a friend will welcome you. For such is the Christian charity of the Lord, expressions of which have sweetened my life during my ten years' sojourn in Bulgaria. (Balducci, pp. 168–169)

Pause: Ask yourself, What does it mean to be "more than merely Christian" in my life?

Pope John's Words

Today more than ever, certainly more than in previous centuries, we are called to serve man as such, and not merely Catholics; to defend above all and everywhere the rights of the human person, and not merely those of the Catholic Church. Today's world, the needs made plain in the last fifty years, and a deeper understanding of doctrine have brought us to a new situation, as I said in my opening speech to the Council. It is not that the

Gospel has changed: it is that we have begun to understand it better. Those who have lived as long as I have were faced with new tasks in the social order at the start of the century; those who, like me, were twenty years in the East and eight in France, were enabled to compare different cultures and traditions, and know that the moment has come to discern the signs of the times, to seize the opportunity and to look far ahead. (Hebblethwaite, pp. 498–499)

Reflection

The idea that each of us is somehow responsible for all of humanity, for everyone in the human family, seems overwhelming. It seems bigger than us! But Pope John's insight, coming as it did in the early sixties, has had a profound impact on the Christian understanding of the idea of taking responsibility for the world.

We are not called, Pope John was saying, to care only for those who are Christian or who agree to become Christian. We are called to care for all women and men as sisters and brothers. This care is expressed in how we set national priorities, how clearly we speak up for human rights, how we transform Christian parishes into working groups with a focus on local and worldwide justice.

What Pope John suggested is not easy. It is a major commitment on the part of Christians. One might say that when, at our baptism, we promised to reject evil and work for good, this is what we promised to do. We promised, in the Rite of Baptism, to "reject sin so as to live in the freedom of God's children." This is a mighty big promise. It is a lifelong vow, a religious vow if you will, that calls us into the lifestyle Pope John envisioned—one in which all women and men would care for one another. What does it mean to "reject sin" if not to reject selfishness and greed, to reject hatred and division, to reject violence and war?

Only this kind of lifestyle produces "the freedom of God's children." Notice that the baptismal vow does not say "the freedom of Christians." This insight, that we are all members of the family of God, found its way into many of the core documents of Vatican II. It was expressed by Pope John in other writings, especially in *Pacem in Terris*, and it serves as the most important insight for the global village of the twenty-first century.

If Christians have a contribution to make to the welfare of the modern world in this new century, it is a firm belief that all human beings belong to us—because they belong to God.

This is the upshot of Mary's hymn, her Magnificat: for those of good heart and sound life, God is with us. "Your mercy," Mary sang, "is from age to age toward those who fear you." There is a great lesson here for church insiders who think they have a corner on the market of God's grace, those who believe they can somehow determine on whom God's favor will rest. God has "confused the proud in their inmost thoughts," Mary sang, and "deposed the mighty from their thrones and raised the lowly to high places."

God, it seems, stands with those who are weakest in the eyes of this world. Can we dare to do less?

✧ Read a major newspaper and keep a list of all those peoples around the world about whose joys, troubles, griefs, needs, or struggles you know.

✧ Post a map of the world in your home and learn the names of the peoples and nations of the world as they come into your awareness.

✧ Read and study the *Pastoral Constitution on the Church in the Modern World* and the *Declaration on the Relationship of the Church to Non-Christians,* two major documents from Vatican II. What does it mean to be Christian in light of these teachings?

✧ Ask your parish or church council to sponsor a discussion series about how your community can contribute to human welfare, both at home and abroad.

God's Word

My being proclaims your greatness,
and my spirit finds joy in you, God my Savior.

For you have looked upon me, your servant, in my
        lowliness;
all ages to come shall call me blessed.

God, you who are mighty, have done great things for me.
Holy is your name.

Your mercy is from age to age toward those who fear you.

You have shown might with your arm
and confused the proud in their inmost thoughts.

You have deposed the mighty from their thrones
and raised the lowly to high places.

The hungry you have given every good thing
while the rich you have sent away empty.

You have upheld Israel your servant, ever mindful of
      your mercy—

even as you promised our ancestors;
promised Abraham, Sarah, and their descendants forever.

                (Schreck and Leach, p. 16)

Closing prayer:

O God of the day and of the night,
    God of the peoples of the world
    and of our hearts,
        guide us now to embrace one another.
Strengthen our resolve to live out our religious vows
    taken at baptism
    when we promised
    to reject sin
    and embrace charity and justice.
Guide our feet into the way of peace. Amen.

Open Wide Your Arms to All

Theme: It is possible for us to open our arms and our hearts to all, embracing one another in charity and breaking down the barriers that divide us, no matter how great they are.

Opening prayer:

O Great Unifier of humankind,
　　you are the one in whom we find our peace,
　　the one in whom we find our unity.
Grant to us now the spirit of charity
　　as we encounter one another
　　　　in our businesses,
　　　　schools,
　　　　homes,
　　　　and churches,
　　so that we might become one in you
　　through Jesus Christ. Amen.

About Pope John

At the time of John's pontificate, many in the church called for rapid and extensive reform regarding the liturgy, the place of laypeople, the role of bishops in church authority, and the church's place in society. There were also others who believed that few such reforms were needed. These latter believed that what was needed was a stronger assertion of church authority in the face of certain modern theological, liturgical, and intellectual movements.

Pope John had a way of addressing such strong differences, a way that called those who held strong opinions on either side to rise above their stances to an area where such opinions no longer mattered. For example, regarding communists, Pope John made this paradoxical observation: "They are the enemies of the Church, but the Church has no enemies . . ." (Fesquet, p. 123). Monsignor Guerry, Archbishop of Cambrai, offered this insight into this aspect of Pope John's leadership:

> On 3 May last year, in private conversation, the Pope confided to me his grief that so many men of good will in the world thought that the Church rejected and condemned them. Then, showing me the crucifix upon his table, he said with emotion: "But I must be like Christ. I open wide my arms to embrace them. I love them and I am their father. I am always ready to welcome them." Then, turning to me, he said: "Monsignore, all that the Gospel requires of us has not yet been understood." (Balducci, p. 31)

Pope John opened his arms wider than many in the church thought wise, but he did so in the name of learning to understand "all that the Gospel requires." The following story demonstrates how John embraced all and saw God's children in all whom he encountered:

> John XXIII granted an audience to *Izvestia* editor Alexis Adzhubei, [Soviet leader] Khrushchev's son-in-law, who was accompanied by his wife. During the exchange of introductions, the Pope turned to the latter and asked the name of her children.
> "Nikita, Alexis and Ivan!" she replied timidly.
> "Three beautiful names indeed!" exclaimed the Pope who did not fail to point out that Ivan corresponded to his own name, John.

Then he added: "When you get home, give your children, and particularly Ivan, an affectionate pat on the head for me. The others must not take offense at this seeming favoritism."

In a later colloquy with editor Adzhubei, Pope John, according to Monsignor Capovilla, recalled the Biblical passages on the creation of the world, and commented on them as follows: "The first epoch was that of light: *fiat lux.* We are at present in the first era, that of light: the light of my eyes has met with the light of your eyes. May the Lord assist the progress of good if it so pleases Him." (Fesquet, p. 125)

Pause: How do you meet the light of others' eyes? To whom do you struggle to open wide your arms? Who are the ones you are most likely to exclude?

Pope John's Words

One day while walking in the Vatican gardens with his secretary, Monsignor Loris Capovilla, Pope John was listening to some of his recent notes being read in preparation for upcoming work. As he admired the beauty of the sunlight playing off the famous dome of Saint Peter's Basilica, the pope stopped and listened closely to a passage from the writings of Saint John Chrysostom:

"Christ has left us on this earth so that we may become shining beacons and teachers who know how to instruct; so that we may perform our task as angels, that is as messengers to men; so that we may be adults among children, and spiritual men among the worldly, in order to win them over; so that we may be sown as seed, and bear abundant fruit. It would not even be necessary for us to expound our doctrine, if our life were in this way so radiant; it would not be necessary to have recourse to words if our deeds gave such testimony. There would be no pagans if we all behaved like real Christians." There were a few moments of silence. Then the Pope said: "This is the truth. Anyone who asks what are the characteristic lines of my pontificate, may be answered with this or with other similar words. That is all there is to it." (Balducci, pp. 32–33)

Reflection

So often we confine ourselves to narrow thinking about who is welcome at our table. We come to believe that a certain well-defined group of "insiders" who believe as we do are the ones we will welcome. But in throwing open his arms to all, Pope John recklessly opened the doors and windows of the church to all. This changes forever how we develop our "guest list" for who is welcome at the table and who is not.

One of the themes developed by Pope John Paul II for the church as it moved toward the third millennium was that of opening wide the doors to Christ. In this he echoes the hopes and dreams of Pope John. But what does this mean, to open wide the doors, or to open wide our arms to all? How do we take in all people without distinction as sisters and brothers?

It was very much in fashion in the sixties and early seventies to speak about the brotherhood or sisterhood of all. There was a spirit, inaugurated by leaders like Pope John, a spirit of cooperation and inclusivity. We dreamed of racial, national, and ethnic unity. We entered a heady period of ecumenism, of outreach to one another, and of hope for the future as such dialog continued.

But some of the fears that previously divided us, and then diminished for some time, now threaten to divide us again. Some fear we don't follow the rules closely enough, or that we are too ready to accept the beliefs of others. Others fear that there isn't enough "Catholic identity" left in the church, that somehow holding on to sharp differences between Christian churches will benefit the mission of the Gospel. There is a new movement today toward legalism, toward strict boundaries, and toward eliminating those with whom we do not agree.

But many others prefer to recapture the spirit of Pope John, and to say again with him, "all that the Gospel requires of us has not yet been understood."

For those on the Christian spiritual journey, this is a very important matter. In the end we will be judged on how we have treated one another. We should be careful about whom we exclude as potential companions for this journey—sometimes even a tax collector or a public sinner may play a central role in working out our salvation.

✧ In your faith community, who is on the guest list and who is not? Who is invited to the table and who is not? Ask your community to give formal reflection to this question in light of the spirit of Pope John's mission to open his arms and those of the church to all.

✧ What do you most fear will result from a more open policy toward those who are not currently welcomed, passively or actively, to your community table? Talk with a friend about which of these fears is the most prominent for you:
+ fear that the church will be less perfect if everyone is allowed in
+ fear that God will be angry if we loosen our rules
+ fear that "outsiders" will not understand your faith
+ fear that the rule breakers will have a bad effect on others
+ fear that the Gospel will be compromised
+ fear that God doesn't want those others in this church

✧ Search the Gospels from this point of view and develop a description of what you think the attitude of Jesus might have been in this situation. Who would have been on his guest list?

God's Word

As Jesus was walking along, he saw a man called Matthew sitting at the tax booth; and he said to him, "Follow me." And he got up and followed him.

And as he sat at dinner in the house, many tax collectors and sinners came and were sitting with him and his disciples. When the Pharisees saw this, they said to his disciples, "Why does your teacher eat with tax collectors and sinners?" But when he heard this, he said, "Those who are well have no need of a physician, but those who are sick. Go and learn what this means, 'I desire mercy, not sacrifice.' For I have come to call not the righteous but sinners." (Matthew 9:9–13)

Closing prayer:

O Divine Source of love,
  we pray for the grace of openness
  that comes only from you
    so that we might welcome to our tables
    those brothers and sisters
    who do not now belong to us.
Grant us the courage of our convictions
  as we establish your Reign in our times
  and open wide our doors to Christ. Amen.

Don't Take Yourself Too Seriously

Theme: We ought not take ourselves or our positions more seriously than the situation demands. We can rest in the assurance that the One who guides us all never leaves our side.

Opening prayer:

O Divine Guide of our souls,
> develop within me the trust in your presence
> that will enable me to work without worry,
>> to pray without ceasing,
>> and to sleep without distress.
Help me remember as I go about my daily work
> that you remain with me
> in all I say and do. Amen.

About Pope John

John XXIII paid considerable thought to all the problems that faced him. He gave his closest attention to every task or request, no matter how small. More than ever before in his life, John felt the responsibility that had been placed upon him in his position as pope. He did not feel it as a burden, as he often assured those around him, but more as a God-given mission, which he therefore carried out joyfully. For this reason John could surmount almost all difficulties with ease. His goodness used to turn opponents into repentant followers. He could never understand how men who held high office in the church could complain about the burden of their pastoral and official tasks. Once a man is called by the Holy Spirit to be a priest, he used to say, he must assume the responsibility to preach and to practice the love of one's neighbor.

In the first private audience he had been granted, a newly appointed bishop complained to John XXIII that the added burden of his new office prevented him from sleeping. "Oh," said John compassionately, "the very same thing happened to me in the first few weeks of my pontificate, but then one day my guardian angel appeared to me in a daydream and whispered: 'Giovanni, don't take yourself so seriously.' And ever since then I've been able to sleep." (Klinger, p. 85)

Pause: In the work of raising your family, doing your job, volunteering at your parish, or developing a prayer life, do you ever take yourself too seriously? What burdens and heaviness do you carry?

Pope John's Words

The life of a priest in our own times is quite different from what it was in the past, and is exposed to new and seductive temptations: the attraction of positions and offices, and the tendency to a certain acquiescent serenity, with little zeal and little fervour for souls. And so it happens that instead of praying together, to the common edification of the faithful, instead of singing with joy in the light of day, it is easy to be overcome with fatigue; it is easy to find words only to mourn for ourselves and to indulge in complaints about others that are neither charitable nor pious. Oh, what a penance it is to have to live with some of our brethren, who are always talking about what is merely the exterior form of priestly activity and barely conceals an eager anxiety and ambition, not always veiled or modest, for promotions, for higher or more distinguished office: a habit of turning everything into a minor key, thus hastening the preparation of a colourless and wearisome old age. (Balducci, p. 118)

Reflection

When we feel the burden of our commitments, it is difficult for us when someone tells us to "lighten up." We don't want to hear that our problems aren't terrible or that our situation in life isn't the worst. We want the sympathies of others, just as the bishop attending his first meeting with the pope wanted John's sympathy. We easily fall into the habit of considering our work so essential that without it, without *us*, our family, our workplace, or even our parish could not go on.

It is not uncommon to think this way. When we become wrapped up in what we're doing, we often become "sole players," and forget that we are not alone, that we also have, first, the Divine Spirit providing us the grace and energy we need, and second, we have one another. We are not sole players in our work, no matter how lonely or isolated we may feel.

Pope John's perspective on this is very helpful. "Don't take yourself so seriously" is good advice to the overworked, the frustrated, and the sleepless. But it is also good advice to the efficient, the certain, and the anxious. Indeed, Pope John's advice can help us lighten up, even if we feel we don't need to. It is especially good advice for those who are eager for promotions in their work, for those who feel they aren't appreciated enough, or that if they just worked a little harder for their families, their employers, or their parishes, they would be appreciated or rewarded more.

There will always be successes and difficulties. So to focus on the one—boasting of our glories—seems as out of place as to focus on the other—losing sleep because of our troubles.

But how do we cope with more complex and confusing life situations? with the same simple approach taught by this pope? In the face of domestic abuse, downsizing at our workplace, or international terrorism, are we to say, in so many words, "Giovanni, don't take yourself so seriously"?

Well, perhaps this wisdom is not too far from a healthy spiritual course for us to follow, even when the situation is serious and life-threatening. When we have honestly done our part in each of these situations, when we have gone as far as we can go and done what is best for us, then the rest is no longer in our hands. When we reach this point in any given situation, we may well be facing the greatest test of our faith in divine providence.

It is tough for us. We don't want to let go, even after we have done all we can. We want to hang on, to try to push a little harder and do a little more. In the face of these sometimes terrible life situations, we feel the heavy burdens of injustice and hatred, and we believe that by holding on to that, we can force change. In fact, letting go is the way to force change. At the cross, Jesus took all the power into his own hands by forgiving his killers. This hard lesson teaches us that the worst thing is not losing our liberty, our self-determination, or even our life. The worst thing is losing our inner freedom and our soul.

The Greeks used several words to describe the soul, one of which is *psyche*. Used in its usual context, *psyche* means the "being-ness" of a person. It also carries the sense of "lightness of being," and is the same word used in Greek for butterfly. On the other hand, when the Scriptures speak of sin, they often speak of it as a burden, a heaviness we carry with us, the opposite of lightness.

In the story of Bartimaeus in the Gospel of Mark, this is brought to full light for us to see. Bartimaeus (whose name means "son of fear") was unable to see at all, unable to have any perspective, so heavy were his burdens. But when he encountered Christ, he threw off his mantle and joyfully ran after Jesus with the lightness of step you would expect from a youngster. What was this mantle of which Bartimaeus rid himself? What burdens did he throw off his shoulders?

✧ What prevents you from lightening up? Talk with a friend about which of the following statements most truly reflects your attitude when you take yourself too seriously.
+ No one else can do what you do.
+ Only you understand the situation.

✦ There is a terrible moral urgency, brought on by injustice, with which you cannot live.

✦ You harbor memories of harsh words or the loss of love.

✦ You acknowledge a deep and unyielding loneliness within yourself.

✦ You have a sense of responsibility for others.

✧ List the areas in which you feel most out of control. What are the matters that make you sleepless? What do you worry about most?

✧ Reflect carefully on your list in light of the wisdom of Pope John and the Gospel story quoted at the end of this meditation. What elements on that list can you change? Which ones can you not change?

✧ How realistic is the teaching of Jesus in the story of Bartimaeus to us in modern times? What does this text mean to you? Read a commentary on it and consider carefully how this text can inform your own life.

God's Word

They came to Jericho. As he and his disciples and a large crowd were leaving Jericho, Bartimaeus son of Timaeus, a blind beggar, was sitting by the roadside. When he heard that it was Jesus of Nazareth, he began to shout out and say, "Jesus, Son of David, have mercy on me!" Many sternly ordered him to be quiet, but he cried out even more loudly, "Son of David, have mercy on me!" Jesus stood still and said, "Call him here." And they called the blind man, saying to him, "Take heart; get up, he is calling you." So throwing off his cloak, he sprang up and came to Jesus. Then Jesus said to him, "What do you want me to do for you?" The blind man said to him, "My teacher, let me see again." Jesus said to him, "Go; your faith has made you well." Immediately he regained his sight and followed him on the way. (Mark 10:46–52)

Closing prayer:

O Divine Guide for our souls,
    we come to you now in faith,
    asking for the grace of freedom.
Lighten our souls by infusing them with trust
    in your presence and power.
When we have done our part,
    then help us surrender into your care
    the outcomes and the future.
Help us then to discern our part well,
    and give us the strength
    to live according to our faith. Amen.

Living by What We Preach

Theme: Individuals and communities must live according to what they teach and preach.

Opening prayer:

We call on you,
>   great and all-powerful God,
>   to guide us as we go about our daily work,
>   to keep before ourselves
>   the connection between faith and life.
Guide us in keeping clear our own call
>   "to do justice,
>   and to love kindness,
>   and to walk humbly with [our] God" (Micah 6:8).

About Pope John

Pope John enjoyed taking walks in the Vatican gardens. Unlike previous popes though, he did not care to take his walks at prearranged times—he preferred to stroll more spontaneously. Consequently, the practice of clearing the gardens of Vatican staff and workers so that the pope could walk in private could not be undertaken. At first gardeners and other workers would withdraw, getting out of the pope's sight by going so far as to hide behind shrubbery. One day a group of street cleaners saw the pope coming and immediately ran for cover.

The Pope did not enjoy this game of hide-and-seek. "Come out again, all of you," he called out. "I won't do anything to you. I want to talk to you. Come. Hurry up, *avanti, venite!*" Timidly, and very slowly, one after another, they came up to the Pope. He did not let them stay on their knees very long, but instead asked them about their families. After they had all had the chance to boast that they were the fathers of a fairly large number of children, John said, "There were twelve children in our home, too. They are all farmers except myself. Five of them are still living." Then the Pope wanted to know what they received as wages for their work. "What?" he replied, frowning, when they told him that they made only 1,000 lire a day ($1.60). "That's only 24,000 lire a month [$38.40]. No family with lots of children can live on that. What has become of justice? Just wait, we'll change that."

The Pope turned around and went immediately to his study to investigate. First he canceled the contract with the Roman firm which, in a written agreement for the cleaning and maintenance of Vatican streets also stipulated the small salaries given the workers. Considering the fees mentioned in the contract, the company certainly should have been able to pay higher wages.

This marked the beginning of a general review of all wage and salary scales in the Vatican. The lowest wages were doubled, while the higher ones were increased in a gradually decreasing scale, so that today the wages and salaries in the Vatican are significantly higher than those in the rest of Italy. At the same time, the Pope ordered that for each child a man had, he should receive an extra monthly allowance of 10,000 lira. It is not surprising that Roman workers now compete for jobs in the Vatican, which only recently they scorned. (Klinger, pp. 47–48)

Pause: We often find preaching, teaching, or witnessing to the Gospel a comfortable way to place a bit of distance between our own life choices and the expectations we have of others. What gaps exist in your own life between what you claim to believe and how you actually live?

Pope John's Words

We cannot always require others to observe the Church's teaching on social justice if we do not apply it in our own domain. The Church must take the lead in social justice by its own good example. (Klinger, p. 48)

Reflection

After talking with the street cleaners, Pope John could have delivered a speech on the great need for reform in the ancient Vatican City administration. He could have spoken eloquently about the need for better wages, the call for justice from the Scriptures, and the terrible living conditions of the workers. But had he done so, very little might have ever been accomplished. Such a papal speech, while theologically correct and even understandable, would have added a layer of needless complexity to the situation. It most likely would have forestalled any real action.

Instead, he simply took the first small step and *acted according to his beliefs*. For many people who are active in the church, doing as Pope John did presents a great challenge. We become so involved with our work, whether as paid or volunteer workers, that we lose sight of the source of our faith. We lose touch with the Maker of the universe. We forget that the spirit of Jesus remains with us today. Our busy-ness substitutes for prayerfulness.

This is the story of the liturgy coordinator who talks more about God than with God. He or she becomes so committed to liturgical principles and forms that the simple expressions of faith that emerge from everyday life no longer seem adequate. This is the story of parish volunteers whose work overtakes their faith. They spend so much time volunteering that they lose sight of family, neighborhood, and personal life. It is the story of the religious educator who has not incorporated into his or her own life the very matters of faith being taught. It is the story of the pastor who has not tended his own soul very well recently. He recommends rest, prayer, retreats, or vacations to others, but doesn't take them himself.

It is the story of any one of us when we fail to live according to our beliefs.

✧ Consider what prevents you from connecting your faith with your everyday life. Where do you find gaps?

✧ What steps would you need to take to make the connection between faith and life more firm? How would you have to change your lifestyle, and your "workstyle," in order to live according to your beliefs?

✧ Make a list of the small steps you can take, the simple ways you can address these changes in lifestyle. Or it may be that you need to follow Pope John's lead in taking bold steps to change certain behaviors.

God's Word

Do not judge, so that you may not be judged. For with the judgment you make you will be judged, and the measure you give will be the measure you get. Why do you see the speck in your neighbor's eye, but do not notice the log in your own eye? Or how can you say to your neighbor, "Let me take the speck out of your eye," while the log is in your own eye? You hypocrite, first take the log out of your own eye, and then you will see clearly to take the speck out of your neighbor's eye. (Matthew 7:1–5)

Closing prayer:

O God, we know that you are with us
    and that all we do is in your eternal care.
Grant us the insight to recognize
    how we can live more closely to our beliefs.
Help us connect our faith in you
        with our daily lives
        so that our judgments of one another
        will be fair. Amen.

Holy Optimism

Theme: We are called to develop an inner sense of optimism about the times in which we live, drawn from our belief that the Holy Spirit speaks in our life.

Opening prayer:

O Divine Source of wisdom and insight,
    help us to trust in the Spirit
    who is active in our midst.
Teach us to discern what is of you
    so that we might follow it earnestly
    and trust in it fully. Amen.

About Pope John

On being elected pope, John was very conscious that he had a rare opportunity to assist the peoples of the world to live together in peace and to advance the cause of the Gospels. He strongly desired that his pontificate be one known for compassion and the open arms of Christ to the world, on which he meditated daily.

The idea of calling a council was entirely consistent with Pope John's desires for the church and the world. Such a council would be the twenty-first such gathering in the history of the church, and it seemed to John to be a way to meet his desires. But the idea for a council did not come to John in a sudden, private revelation. Rather it arose over a period of time, with proper discernment and development.

For many years in Rome, since the beginning of the reign of Pope Pius XII in 1939, there had been talk of a council. Early in his own pontificate, Pope John had talked about it with a few close advisers. Some were in favor of it, others opposed. John kept the idea top secret for several months, speaking only to those who could help him discern if the idea for a council was of God, and not an ego trip of his own. He wished to submit to the Lord's will, and took great care in discernment.

He had learned to test ideas that came to him in prayer, and when tested and found to be of God, to trust them and to organize his life around them. He knew self-deception was possible, even for the pope, and was careful not to allow that to become a factor. Ideas, for Pope John, were to be evaluated according to their persistence and the inner sense of rightness and peace they produced.

The idea of calling a council passed the test. Despite the difficulties and hard work it entailed for him at his age, he trusted God's plan. He saw the calling of the Council as one of the "great graces bestowed on a man who has a low esteem of himself but receives good inspiration and humbly and trustfully proceeds to put them into practice" (*Journal of a Soul*, p. 325).

Pause: How does God speak to you in prayer? How do you discern the voice of God in the din of modern "voices"?

Pope John's Words

In the daily exercise of Our pastoral office, it sometimes happens that We hear certain opinions which disturb Us—opinions expressed by people who, though fired with a commendable zeal for religion, are lacking in sufficient prudence and judgment in their evaluation of events. They can see nothing but calamity and disaster in the present state of the world. They say over and over that this modern age of ours, in comparison with past ages, is definitely deteriorating. One would think from their attitude that history, that great teacher of life, had taught them nothing. They seem to imagine that in the days of the earlier councils everything was as it should be so far as doctrine and morality and the Church's rightful liberty were concerned.

We feel that We must disagree with these prophets of doom, who are always forecasting worse disasters, as though the end of the world were at hand.

Present indications are that the human family is on the threshold of a new era. We must recognize here the hand of God, who, as the years roll by, is ever directing men's efforts, whether they realize it or not, towards the fulfillment of the inscrutable designs of His providence, wisely arranging everything, even adverse human fortune, for the Church's good. (*The Encyclicals*, pp. 426–427)

Reflection

Discernment and trust—for the Christian these are the keys to advancing in the spiritual life. Both require that we first remove ourselves just a little from the picture so that we can hear the voice of God in the events, people, and liturgies that surround us and in the intuitions and emotions that are within us. Ideas come to us, seemingly out of nowhere. Be they large and full of effects, or small and nearly private, they arise within us. They often begin as a seed, one small aspect of a thought appearing in our thinking. They grow to maturity over time and become the agenda of our work and life.

For Pope John the idea that God is with us, intimately a part of our everyday life and the source of knowledge and wisdom, came from his childhood in Sotto il Monte in northern Italy. There he was taught from his earliest years to trust that God does indeed move us, does touch us with God's own word. Reading the journal of his life, one cannot escape noticing the continual growth in Pope John toward trusting more and more in the providence of God.

And so for all of us. Learning to discern God's word in our life and, having discerned it, to organize our life around it, is a practiced spiritual skill. Basic to Pope John's skill was his accompanying optimism about how God is carrying out God's work among us. He knew that God would guide him. There was no doubt. And he knew that, despite what some had to say, these times, in comparison with past ones, were *not* worse. These times were *not* filled with prevarication and ruin. In fact in John's view, these times were ones in which God was bringing the human family to a new order of shared life on Earth.

When one trusts in God and learns to discern God's voice in the din of modern "voices," one can indeed be optimistic. For if we follow God's way, then what harm can come to us? What can separate us from Christ? How can our work fail to be the same as that of Christ?

✧ Examine the ideas you have had lately—not just major ideas like Pope John's idea to call a council, but ordinary, everyday ideas: to invite someone to your home, to have a talk with your child, to pick up a gift for your spouse, to ask for a new assignment, or to read a certain book. Examine your recent intuitions as well.

✧ How have you treated these ideas and intuitions? How have you discerned them? What ideas and intuitions have you ignored or been too busy to take notice of?

✧ Pause often throughout your day to listen for ideas and intuitions about your home, school, parish, workplace, nation, and world. What do you hear? How do you discern what you hear to be certain it is of God rather than of ego?

✧ Talk with a friend about how you discern God's voice in your life, about how God speaks to you in prayer.

God's Word

Beloved, do not believe every spirit, but test the spirits to see whether they are from God; for many false prophets have gone out into the world. By this you know the Spirit of God: every spirit that confesses that Jesus Christ has come in the flesh is from God, and every spirit that does not confess Jesus is not from God. And this is the spirit of the antichrist, of which you have heard that it is coming; and now it is already in the world. Little children, you are from God, and have conquered them; for the one who is in you is greater than the one who is in the world. They are from the world; therefore what they say is from the world, and the world listens to them. We are from God. Whoever knows God listens to us, and whoever is not from God does not listen to us. From this we know the spirit of truth and the spirit of error.

Beloved, let us love one another, because love is from God; everyone who loves is born of God and knows God. Whoever does not love does not know God, for God is love. God's love was revealed among us in this way: God sent his only Son into the world so that we might live through him. (1 John 4:1–9)

Closing prayer:

O Great Divine Spirit of truth,
> you dwell within us at all times,
> guiding us to test the word we hear
> to clarify your voice.
Guide our ears to hear you more clearly
> and our eyes to see you.
Guide our hearts to find you in the din
> of modern life.
Give us the grace to hear your word,
> the wisdom to discern it,
> and the courage to follow it. Amen.

Simplicity of Heart and Speech

Theme: Amid the complexities of modern life, simplicity of heart and speech allow us to concentrate on what is really important: truth, justice, and charity—above all charity.

Opening prayer:

O Maker of the universe
    and Source of all that is,
      grant us simplicity of mind and conduct
      so that others may see in us
      their clear way to you.
Create in us a desire to live in your light
      without pretense,
      foolish words,
      or defensive posturing. Amen.

About Pope John

Enormous confusion and excitement surround a newly elected pope. He immediately becomes the public person all the world sees. Within an hour of his election, the crowd waiting in Saint Peter's Square, and all the world, meet him for the first time.

After his election the new Pope John gave his blessing to those around him and received the homage of the cardinals of the church. He then came to the central *loggia* of Saint Peter's to meet the crowds, who greeted him with great enthusiasm and a noisy throng of flashing lights and cameras. Afterward he tried to describe how he felt at that moment, giving us an insight into the simplicity of heart that he sought for his spiritual journey:

> I remembered Jesus' warning: "Learn of me, for I am meek and humble of heart." Dazzled by the television lights, I could see nothing but an amorphous, swaying mass. I blessed Rome and the world as though I were a blind man. As I came away I thought of all the cameras and lights that from now on, at every moment, would be directed on me. And I said to myself: if you don't remain a disciple of the gentle and humble Master, you'll understand nothing even of temporal realities. Then you'll be really blind. (Hebblethwaite, pp. 287–288)

Pope John almost immediately demonstrated practical ways in which he, as pope, would manifest the meekness and humility Jesus called for. Within a few days of his election, for example, he sent for the editor of the Vatican newspaper:

> The Pope . . . gave him a few suggestions on editorial style. "We would like to see less antique formality in your references to us," Pope John said. "Instead of phrases like, 'the Supreme Pontiff,' or 'the illuminated Holy Father,' or 'we gathered from the august lips,' please simply say, 'The Pope or the Pontiff did so and so.'" (Hatch, p. 183)

Pause: How might your life be simplified? How can you develop and retain simplicity in heart and speech?

Pope John's Words

> Everyone must be treated with respect, prudence and evangelical simplicity.

It is commonly believed and considered fitting that even the everyday language of the Pope should be full of mystery and awe. But the example of Jesus is more closely followed in the most appealing simplicity, not dissociated from the God-given prudence of wise and holy men. Wiseacres may show disrespect, if not scorn, for the simple man. But those wiseacres are of no account; even if their opinions and conduct inflict some humiliations, no notice should be taken of them at all: in the end everything ends in their defeat and confusion. The "simple, upright, God-fearing man" is always the worthiest and the strongest. Naturally he must always be sustained by a wise and gracious prudence. He is a simple man who is not ashamed to profess the Gospel, even in the face of men who consider it to be nothing but weakness and childish nonsense, and to profess it entirely, on all occasions, and in the presence of all; he does not let himself be deceived or prejudiced by his fellows, nor does he lose his peace of mind, however they may treat him. (*Journal of a Soul*, p. 309)

Reflection

How easy it is for us in the spiritual journey to lose our heads! To forget who we really are and to begin to think that we are someone else, that we "become" our title or position. Pope John taught, though, that it is necessary for us to always remember that the simpler, softer approach is closest to that of Jesus.

Often when we take on the work of a new position, whatever that might be—pope, bishop, manager, teacher, parent—we tend to think of ourselves as due a new level of respect from those around us. We easily become pretentious, taking on airs and acting as though the world owes us something special because of who we have now become.

But read again the words of Pope John in this meditation. The real strength of the Christian comes not from dominating others with authority and a sharp tongue but from living in a state of "appealing simplicity" and knowing that all we are and all we have comes not from our own doing but from God.

Many people fear that they will appear weak if they take this approach. If their salary isn't the highest, if their power isn't enforced, if their opinions don't dominate, they feel of less worth. The world argues that we should assert ourselves and take control. But the Gospel calls us to be meek and humble, to remember that we emerge from dust and are filled with the Divine Spirit.

Sometimes, even for those on the spiritual journey, this great desire to assert ourselves by way of our power or position causes us to be dishonest about our actual place. We pretend to be more well placed, more well connected, or more well informed than we really are. We boast of our successes and hide our failures. We speak with a level of certainty unwarranted by what we know or can actually do. In short, we pretend to be more than we are.

In fact, as Pope John taught and demonstrated, we ought to take the opposite road. We ought to act according to our real and actual place in life. And even when that places us in a position of authority, we must treat everyone respectfully.

In his opening speech at Vatican II, Pope John encoded this approach into church history forever. In speaking about how we are to treat those who disagree with us, or those who appear to be outside our faith community, he said that the church has historically opposed errors and dealt with them severely. The church of Pope John's day, by contrast, "prefers the balm of mercy to the arm of severity. She believes that present needs are best served by explaining more fully the purport of her doctrines, rather than by publishing condemnations" (*The Encyclicals*, p. 431).

Let us respectfully take our stand, he was saying, and give those who believe differently the benefit of the doubt, rather than coming down on them with harsh condemnations. Let us look to where we can treat one another with love, rather than looking to those things that divide us, he said in essence. Let us, in other words, reduce even our differences to the simplest level and find in them the possibility of mercy toward one another and love for all as sisters and brothers.

For who among us is the greatest? Who is the most right? Who carries the most power? The most authority? Is it not the one who is most humble, who is most supple in allowing God's spirit to guide us?

✧ Identify situations in which you find people "putting on airs" and making themselves or their positions more important than they really are.

✧ When have you done this yourself?

✧ Invite groups in which you are a member to take this approach: to look for the common ground, to simplify situations of conflict. Seek out others who also wish to take this approach.

✧ Think of ways to reconcile the Gospel value of humility with the modern tendency to assert oneself.

God's Word

A soft answer turns away wrath,
　　but a harsh word stirs up anger.
The tongue of the wise dispenses knowledge,
　　but the mouths of fools pour out folly.
　　　　　　　　　　　　　(Proverbs 15:1–2)

Closing prayer:

O Jesus, meek and humble of heart,
　　teach us wisdom.
Help us to see ourselves as we really are
　　and to offer one another understanding,
　　　　　mercy,
　　　　　and gentleness.
Awaken within us your grace of discipleship
　　so that we might follow Jesus,
　　be filled with the spirit of humility,
　　and allow God to guide us in love. Amen.

Read Little but Well

Theme: With so much information available to us, it is necessary for us to limit what we take in so that we may maintain clarity of spirit.

Opening prayer:

O Divine Source of all knowledge,
　　　guide us in our discernment
　　　as we choose at what level to take in
　　　　　and absorb
　　　　　all the information available to us today.
Be in our hearts and on our minds
　　　as we balance silence,
　　　　　reading,
　　　　　listening,
　　　　　watching,
　　　　　and writing,
　　　so that we might achieve balance and lasting wisdom. Amen.

About Pope John

In his seminary years in Rome, Angelo Roncalli was already aware of the many demands made on us as modern people.

The notes in his journal during this time show him to be on the lookout for distractions from the spiritual journey. He wanted to avoid becoming "too full" of the material around him, fearing that then there would no longer be any room for Christ. During these years he kept his journal faithfully as a way to monitor his growth and record his more intimate thoughts about the challenge of living according to the teachings of Jesus.

This journal, now famous, served Pope John as a monitor in his spiritual growth. It shows a man determined to adopt the way of Jesus as his own way, to avoid the pitfalls of political ambition and pretension. It is an intimate portrayal of Pope John's lifelong desire to allow the Spirit to work through him, to use his life for the good of the world.

Among the ways John sought this balance was in how much media he took in. He feared that too much would distract him, but that too little would fail to afford him the wisdom of the ages. At the age of only twenty-two, he wrote:

> Yesterday my learned Professor of Church history gave us excellent advice, particularly useful to me: read little, little but well. And what he said about reading I will apply to everything else: little but well. When I think of all the books I have read in the course of my studies, in the vacations and during my military service! the tomes, periodicals, newspapers! And how much do I remember of all this? Nothing, or almost nothing. All those spiritual works, all those lives of the saints—and what do I remember? Nothing, or almost nothing. (*Journal of a Soul*, p. 105)

Pause: Consider in how many ways the media is active and how much information is available to you in a single day.

Pope John's Words

> I feel a restless longing to know everything, to study all the great authors, to familiarize myself with the scientific movement in its various manifestations, but in actual fact

I read one book, devour another, and do not get very far with anything. "Give up trying to know too much, for this is very distracting and may lead you astray." (*Journal of a Soul*, p. 105)

Reflection

Modern life is so complex! The options are so many and the information so abundant that it is difficult to choose, much less to cope, with all that lies before us. We live in a media age where family homes now have access to hundreds of television channels and anyone can go to the Internet and obtain information about virtually everything. You might say that we know too much! We have too much information to sort it all out and retain what is most important.

Many people are surrounded by noise at all times. There's a radio or television playing. There's the incessant noise of traffic and airplanes. There's the hum of the shopping mall, complete with the drone of piped-in music. Silence is hard to come by in this busy, racing culture.

Not only that, we have a tremendous awareness of the rest of the world. We have more information than we want or could ever use. We are aware of the difficulties and sufferings of peoples from around the world, made plain to us in the daily news. And the Internet now connects us to places on the other side of the world where we would otherwise never have gone. The amount of information we take in while reading one daily issue of the *New York Times* is more than the amount of information taken in by an average person in the seventeenth century in his or her entire lifetime!

This complexity can drive us to complacency. When the options are so many, we become numb to them all. Or we begin to think either that nothing matters or that everything matters equally.

Where is the Christian journey in all this? Pope John, long before this noisy onslaught of information had reached its contemporary pitch, understood the importance of choosing carefully what we read and hear. His wisdom, to read little but well, challenges us to reorganize what we allow in our midst.

It suggests that we take more control over the media that enters our homes or offices. And, most important, it advises us to be *intentional* about our choices, selecting only those things that enhance our lives and the lives of our families.

Part of the reason for the modern onslaught of noise and media is our discomfort with silence. Silence is more than the absence of sound. In a sense, silence is the fullness of life. Silence is the norm, not the exception. Sounds rise up in silence and ebb away again. But silence remains. Many people fear their own thoughts, which rise in them when silence is present. One poet wrote, "Whenever there is silence around me, by day or night, I am startled by a cry! The first time I heard it I went out and searched and found a man in the throes of crucifixion." Silence can lead us to places we would not otherwise choose to go. It can be that time in which God speaks most clearly to us, and God's word is often upsetting in our modern, planned, and predictable lives.

In the end it is only when we allow silence to well up around us that we are in touch with an inborn human longing, the longing for God. The psalmist wrote that like the deer that longs for running streams, so do our souls long for God.

✧ Make a list of all your information options. Consider each aspect of your life (home, work, hobbies, parenting, and so on) and determine how many ways you can get information and participate in the media.

✧ Take this list into meditation with you and carefully identify those which most edify you and your spiritual journey.

✧ Talk with other people about what articles, books, tapes, videos, or other forms of media have most helped them in their spiritual journeys. Develop a list of those things you would like to add to your life, and also a list of those things you would like to skip over.

✧ Pause to remember times of silence you have had recently. When were they? How did they feel? Take a moment right now to have silence. Are you comfortable with it, or do you prefer noise?

✧ Talk with a friend about which of the following statements best describes you:

+ I want to know about everything in order to be complete.
+ I want to know only what others need and want.
+ I want to know only those things that will make me successful.
+ Knowledge about my inner, emotional life is most important to me.
+ I collect details, and want to know as much as possible.
+ I want to know all the rules and follow them precisely.
+ Facts, schmacts—all I want is to dream.
+ The more information I have, the more I can control it.
+ All this information gathering is just too much work.

God's Word

O God, you are my God whom I eagerly seek;
for you my flesh longs and my soul thirsts
like the earth, parched, lifeless, and without water.
I have gazed toward you in the sanctuary
to see your power and your glory.
For your love is better than life;
my lips shall glorify you.
Thus will I praise you while I live;
lifting up my hands, I will call upon your name.
As with the riches of a banquet shall my soul be filled,
and with exultant lips my mouth shall praise you.

(Psalm 63:1–5)

Closing prayer:

O God, we long for you;
    even in the midst of all other longings,
    we seek you with all our heart.
Now teach us wisdom
    to know well the ways of this world
    so we will be able to choose
from among the many good things around us
    that which is better for us. Amen.

Die Well

Theme: We are called to embrace death, to live within its boundaries, and to pass through it to eternal life.

Opening prayer:

O Divine Source and end of life,
>   be with us as we move through life
>   toward death.
Allow us the grace to see you clearly
>   and to desire eternal union with you
>   as we approach the moment when life ends on Earth
>   and begins in Heaven. Amen.

About Pope John

Even though the official Vatican spokesperson refused to admit it, by the end of May 1963, everyone knew that Pope John lay dying. Reports circulated around the world, and people from far and wide kept vigil in Saint Peter's Square. Pope John had touched so many, Catholic and non-Catholic—they knew that he loved them no matter who they were or what they believed.

By 28 May 1963, John's pain was tremendous as he struggled against his cancer. But that morning he felt somewhat better, and two of his assistants read to him from the countless get-well messages from around the world, from the famous and the ordinary. Shortly after noon he dictated a reply to his well-wishers:

> Since everyone is praying for the sick pope, it's only natural they should have an intention: if God wants the sacrifice of my life, let it be of some use in calling down copious blessings on the ecumenical Council, the Church and on humanity that so longs for peace; but if it pleases the Lord to prolong my pontifical ministry, then let it be for the sanctification of my soul and of all those who work and suffer with me to extend the kingdom of Our Lord. (Hebblethwaite, p. 500)

By 31 May Pope John's doctors agreed there was nothing more they could do to prolong his life. Monsignor Capovilla, his faithful secretary, broke the news to him that the end was at hand. Pope John asked only that he be aided to die with grace. Slowly he met in farewell audience with his family and staff, one after the other, ebbing into and out of sometimes painful and sometimes peaceful sleep.

At 11:00 a.m. on 31 May, Pope John addressed those keeping closest vigil with him. He said, in part:

> The secret of my ministry is in that crucifix you see opposite my bed. It's there so that I can see it in my first waking moment and before going to sleep. It's there, also, so that I can talk to it during the long evening hours. Look at it, see it as I see it. Those open arms have been the programme of my pontificate: they say that Christ died for all, for all. No one is excluded from his love, from his forgiveness.
>
> What did Christ leave to his Church? He left us *"ut omnes unum sint"* [that all may be one: John 10.16] . . .
>
> For my part, I'm not aware of having offended anyone, but if I have, I beg their forgiveness; and if you know anyone who has not been edified by my attitudes or actions, ask them to have compassion on me and to forgive me. In this last hour I feel calm and sure that my Lord, in his mercy, will not reject me. Unworthy though I am, I wanted to serve him, and I've done my best to pay

homage to truth, justice, charity, and the *cor mitis et humilis* [the meek and humble heart] of the Gospel.

My time on earth is drawing to a close. But Christ lives on and the Church continues his work. Souls, souls. *Ut unum sint! ut unum sint!* (Hebblethwaite, pp. 501–502)

On the night of Pentecost, the second of June, twenty thousand young people in Milan stood vigil for Pope John in the Cathedral there. Cardinal Montini, who would soon become Pope Paul VI, was with them. Montini addressed the vigil, emphasizing the need to "gather up his inheritance and his final message of peace." Montini also asserted, "Perhaps never before in our time . . . has a human word—the word of a master, a leader, a prophet, a pope—rung out so loudly and won such affection throughout the whole world" (Hebblethwaite, p. 503).

Crowds continued to gather in Saint Peter's Square, praying for the priest, pope, prophet. In the early morning of 3 June, Pope John awoke and said twice with great emphasis, "Lord, you know that I love you." Throughout the day the crowd in Saint Peter's, as if under a spell, continued to grow. As evening came Mass was celebrated. Inside, at the pope's bedside, members of John's family and staff stood vigil.

They say the prayers for the dying while the Mass proceeds in the square. Towards 7:45 the Mass is over. In the Pope's bedroom, the words of dismissal, *Ite Missa Est*, can be clearly heard over the microphone. Pope John gives a last shudder. His breathing becomes faint and, after a barely audible death-rattle, stops. The doctors bow reverently and shrug. It is 7:49 p.m. (Hebblethwaite, p. 504)

Pause: What do you hope for at the time of your death?

Pope John's Words

It is an indisputable truth that all of us one day will receive a visit from our Sister Death, as St. Francis of Assisi called her. She sometimes presents herself in a sudden and unexpected manner. But we shall remain tranquil, or better undisturbed, if our tree has known how to yield its fruits. He who has worked well, departs when the day has ended. (Fesquet, p. 184)

O Lord, we are now in the evening of our life. I am in my seventy-sixth year. Life is a great gift from our heavenly Father. Three-quarters of my contemporaries have passed over to the far shore. So I too must always be ready for the great moment. The thought of death does not alarm me. Now one of my five brothers also has gone before me, and he was the youngest but one, my beloved Giovanni. Ah, what a good life and what a fine death! My health is excellent and still robust, but I cannot count on it. I want to hold myself ready to reply *adsum* [I am here] at any, even the most unexpected moment. (*Journal of a Soul*, p. 291)

Reflection

Pope John desired to live on to see the work of the Second Vatican Council completed. He did not desire death. But when he realized that no more could be done to improve his medical condition, he welcomed Sister Death. He had lived his entire life as though death might call him at any time; he kept before him always his mission to offer the world the love of Christ.

Christians are called to live like this, called to allow death to define life. Just as the edge of your desk shapes what your desk looks like, gives it limit and form, so death shapes life. It is our ultimate limit. It defines who we are and how we live. Indeed it may well be that the patterns of light or darkness with which we live follow us into death and remain with us eternally.

An excellent way for us to develop a healthy "death consciousness" is to live in such a way that our lives are complete each evening when we go to our bed. Each evening, when we examine our day, we might turn to those whom we have harmed and ask forgiveness. And each evening we might forgive any who have harmed us in any way. Thus we empty our souls of sin in the evening hours, inviting the Holy Spirit to dwell there instead. We are warned not to go to bed with anger, fear, or aggression, but instead to have in our heart only thoughts of love, courage, and gentleness.

The evening prayer known as Compline expresses how our life comes to a daily pause at bedtime: "Protect us, Lord, as we stay awake, watch over us as we sleep, that awake, we may keep watch with Christ, and asleep, rest in his peace."

✧ Form the habit of reviewing each day before sleep, remembering all whom you have encountered in person, by telephone, through e-mail, or in any other way. Think of the strangers you have met, the friends with whom you have spent time, and the household in which you live. Think too of those whom you have not called or written, of those who may be waiting to hear from you.

✧ Develop a system of keeping your conscience clear by freely forgiving others and by asking for forgiveness when needed.

✧ Do not let the sun go down on your anger.

✧ Institute a form of Compline in your life. Whether alone or with your household, spend a few moments at the end of the day committing yourself anew to Christ, preparing your soul for sleep, and drawing your day to a suitable close.

✧ If you knew you were to die soon, who would you call to reconcile or to deepen ties? How would your awareness of impending death change your life?

✦ Would you work to complete everything you have on your plate?
✦ Would you make sure all those around you were cared for?
✦ Would you be certain to bring all your work to a successful conclusion?
✦ Would you sink into melancholy, weeping with your sadness?
✦ Would you study death and the afterlife, seeking to understand as much about them as possible?
✦ Would you carefully examine your conscience?

- ✦ Would you party away the rest of your life, seeking to fill life to its maximum before death?
- ✦ Would you fight your impending death, seeking to over-power it and prevent it?
- ✦ Would you simply shut down all systems and wait for death to arrive?

God's Word

And now I am no longer in the world, but they are in the world, and I am coming to you. Holy Father, protect them in your name that you have given me, so that they may be one, as we are one. (John 17:11)

Closing prayer:

O Sister Death,
    grant us a peaceful death
    after a life filled with love.
Prepare us daily to embrace you,
    ready at any moment
    to fall into God's eternal arms.
O Divine Guide of our souls,
    teach us mercy and compassion,
    teach us forgiveness and humility.
May we forever live with you in eternal love. Amen.

Holy Folly

Theme: Humor and unpredictability help to create a healthy spiritual life. Everything is not so serious that we should not have a little fun now and then.

Opening prayer:

O Spirit of joy,
> grant us the ability to surprise ourselves
> even as you surprise us
> with the places your wind blows
> and the hearts your love ignites with fire!
Develop the freedom in our souls
> to depart from expectations long enough
> to dally in the liberty of your Spirit. Amen.

About Pope John

Pope John was quite convinced that the strict guardians of Vatican protocol did not approve of his ways of expressing himself, which did not always conform to diplomatic conventions. He had a quick and surprising wit, and often seemed to act on the spur of the moment.

On January 20, 1959, the Pope got into his car with the apparent intention of driving as usual to the Vatican

Gardens. Instead, the driver swung the car around St. Peter's Square and disappeared into the Roman traffic without benefit of an escort. Nobody knew where the Pope had gone; Vatican officials were frantic; the civil authorities of Rome and, in fact, the whole Italian Government were in a panic. What would the world say if something happened to the Pope?

Pope John knew that nothing would happen to him. He just wanted to see some old friends. Word had reached him that Father Joseph Bergeron of Canada, who managed a Home for old and retired Holy Cross priests, had wanted to see him, but had not asked for an audience because "A humble priest like me should not take up the Holy Father's time." The Pope's car beat its way through the traffic-clogged streets to the old priests' Home on Monte Mario. There, while the Vatican officials answered hundreds of telephone calls with the helpless words, "We don't know where he's gone," and security police rocketed around Rome searching fruitlessly, Pope John, having refused the big throne-like chair they offered him, sat in a rocker in a circle of twenty-two very happy old gentlemen, having a lovely time gossiping away the afternoon. (Hatch, pp. 218–219)

Pause: When was the last time you did something that surprised everyone who knows you? Is it about time you tried it again?

Pope John's Words

Without a little holy folly the Church will not enlarge her tabernacles. (Balducci, p. 111)

Reflection

One requirement for living the Gospel is the willingness to be unpredictable. If the Holy Spirit has one characteristic upon which all can agree, it is that no one can predict where and when it will turn up. No one knows where it comes from or where it is going. The spiritual woman or man finds in her or his soul a supple nature, an ability to bend, to change with the circumstances.

Comedy and unpredictability are closely matched virtues. One depends upon the other to work. And both spring from the heart of a person having fun with work or life. They rise from someone so confident in his or her situation and place that laughter is possible. Only a person of deep faith, of profound trust in the unfolding of life's pathways, can be so confident.

But we resist this bending and shaping, don't we? We prefer the predictable, the sure, the tried and true. We prefer to celebrate Christmas "just as we did last year," or to do a particular task a certain way "because it's always been done that way."

We also tend to be very serious. We have so much to get done, we say, so there's no time to fool around. A given situation is serious, we insist, and nothing to laugh at. We find ourselves trudging through our daily life, unable to pause and consider what's happening, unable to seek humor in any of it. The papacy is one of the most serious and, in terms of protocol, predictable offices in the world. Protocol and pomp are laid out in detailed books of rubrics, the traditions remain unbroken, and the patterns of behavior for popes laid down in the late sixteenth century dominate. Into this scene Pope John introduced an element of surprise and comedy. This was in stark contrast to his predecessors, especially the very serious and formal Pope Pius XII.

One can hardly imagine laughter ringing in the halls of the Vatican. But John added laughter and surprise. And what did this add to his papacy? You might say this warmer, more supple style was key to his work there. You might even say that his humanness and genuine love of others was shown in his willingness to break any rule for the comfort of his guests—you might say that this feature "made" his papacy.

Pope John encouraged us to live a more joyous Christianity—not by reducing its demands on us but by setting us free from "old age" and returning us to the great joy that comes from mutual love. Fear, anger, and aggression were all out of place in John's papacy, and were replaced by trust, joy, and a willingness to make light of our differences.

How different would our own homes and workplaces be, our parishes and schools, if we took the same approach! How much lighter our load in life would be if we sought the comic side of it all. How much more love we would share with one another if we were more willing to make light of differences. And how much more fun it would all be for us if there were surprises now and then!

✧ What has surprised you recently? What patterns in your own life might you change in order to surprise those around you?

✧ Think about those who make you laugh in your everyday life. How do these people affect your workplace, home, or parish?

✧ Talk with a friend about which of these is the greatest obstacle to laughter in your own life:
+ Your busy-ness and the drive for perfection
+ The great needs of others you feel obliged to meet
+ Your own drive for success and your fear of failure
+ Your melodramatic approach to life's situations that keeps you from enjoying life fully
+ Your serious approach to life, which buries you in details
+ Your strong sense of loyalty to those with authority and their rules that prevent you from lightening up
+ Your role as a disappointed optimist
+ Your own drive to be in complete control that shapes your demand for predictability
+ Your life's burdens that are just too overwhelming for you to find humor in anything

✧ Having identified what prevents you from living with surprise, joy, and comedy, outline what steps you might take to change this, to add this dimension to your spirituality.

God's Word

Now there was a Pharisee named Nicodemus, a leader of the Jews. He came to Jesus by night and said to him, "Rabbi, we know that you are a teacher who has come from God; for no one can do these signs that you do apart from the presence of God." Jesus answered him, "Very truly, I tell you, no one can see the kingdom of God without being born from above." Nicodemus said to him, "How can anyone be born after having grown old? Can one enter a second time into the mother's womb and be born?" Jesus answered, "Very truly, I tell you, no one can enter the kingdom of God without being born of water and Spirit. What is born of the flesh is flesh, and what is born of the Spirit is spirit. Do not be astonished that I said to you, 'You must be born from above.' The wind blows where it chooses, and you hear the sound of it, but you do not know where it comes from or where it goes. So it is with everyone who is born of the Spirit." (John 3:1–8)

Closing prayer:

O Divine Spirit,
 Unpredictable Force of life,
 Surprising Shaper of our journeys,
  offer us the warmth of humor
  and the confidence of joy in your providence.
Grant us the ability to see ourselves
 in light of your own great designs for us,
 and to trust that life is unfolding as it should.
Loosen our wit within us,
 and give us the spirit of holy folly. Amen.

Youthfulness of Spirit

Theme: Youthfulness of spirit allows us to open the windows of our hearts and institutions to let in the fresh air of the Holy Spirit.

Opening prayer:

O Divine Guide of life,
    help us to see you as you really are,
        desiring always a new springtime in the church
            and in our lives.
Keep us faithful to the Spirit
    who lives within us
        and implants there the urgent freshness and vigor
            of spiritual youthfulness. Amen.

About Pope John

Pope John seemed to have an inborn, youthful optimism about all things, both within the church and outside it. This optimism emerged from a playful presence with all those who came in contact with him. Longtime Vatican insiders considered this a fault. But this new vigor, especially in an eighty-year-old man, opened doors and hearts the world over. Pope John "carried on" with Protestants, Jews, unbelievers, communists, the Eastern churches, and many others previously unwelcome at the Vatican. He behaved as though we had nothing to fear from anyone and as though God might choose anyone to deliver God's message.

John likewise looked to the early youthful years of the church, those first centuries when the church was more fervently animated by the spirit of Jesus. Pope John never fell victim to fear and never stopped believing that God in our age was preparing to do great work, as great as that done during those earliest years of the Christian community.

This showed itself most prominently in John's dealings with the staff of the Curia while preparations were underway for the Council. There, in ways unchanged since the sixteenth century, officials protected age-old ways of understanding the church and their roles in it. Pope John worked patiently but insistently to add a youthfulness of spirit to their view. He dreamed of a new springtime for the church. Despite the resistance of these Vatican insiders, Pope John persisted.

One day, for example, shortly after Pope John had announced his intention to hold Vatican II, a faithful prelate of the Curia came to see him. This prelate was of the opinion that it might require ten to twenty years of preparation to get Vatican II ready, so he told the pope, "It is absolutely impossible to open the Council in 1963."

"Pope John replied: 'Fine, we'll open it in 1962!'" (Fesquet, p. 156). And indeed the council opened in October 1962.

In Pope John's opening speech at the Council itself, he emphasized his view that the time was upon us for spring to break forth:

> For with the opening of this Council a new day is dawning on the Church, bathing her in radiant splendor. It is yet the dawn, but the sun in its rising has already set our heats aglow. All around is the fragrance of holiness and joy. (*The Encyclicals*, p. 434)

Pause: What "age-old" opinions do you hold about how things must be done in your life and work?

Pope John's Words

When I think that at my age, [Bishop] Radini was on the point of dying, I am tempted to think of myself as an old man. It is necessary to fight against such feelings; despite outward appearances, youth of mind and spirit must be preserved. For this is pleasing to God, a good example, and helpful to one whose duty it is to communicate joy and optimism to others. . . .

But, thank God, I prefer to look forward rather than back. Even my most cherished memories of persons and of things linger as if to remind me of the reunion which we can expect. Life is rather like a long sea voyage. We say goodbye with tears when leaving those we love—but lo and behold, when we reach our destination they are waiting for us on the quayside. (Algisi, pp. 130–131)

Reflection

How old is God? Most people would answer that God is ageless, but in so saying, some might mean that God is infinitely old. Pope John would most likely have answered that God is infinitely young. To him God's everlasting newness was foremost in leading us to consider how to live our lives and shape our church.

For those on the spiritual journey, this is no small matter! How often have religious people earned the reputation of being stodgy, tiresome, tedious, and uninteresting? The idea of "spring breaking forth," as John described the Second Vatican Council, is the last one most people would associate with being religious.

This attitude comes about because religions sometimes become mired in their traditions, their unchanging formulas, and their hesitancy to accept human nature and experience. Being thoroughly modern is usually not the concern of the church, nor of religious people. In fact mistrust of modern thinking and new social developments has been the hallmark of most religions throughout the world.

But in fact resistance to modernity is often resistance to the Holy Spirit. When we refuse to move forward in religious thinking, we fail to hear the Spirit speaking in our times. When we cling to seventeenth-century models of prayer, social organization, or theology, we abandon the Spirit's work in the lives of people since then. The Spirit doesn't speak only through official channels—and in fact often appears where we least expect to find God present.

Maintaining a youthful openness (Pope John's own desire for himself) allows us to trust that God is revealed to us all the time. It allows us to listen to how the Spirit speaks in everyday life. This is what makes us the salt of the earth. This is what makes us the light of the world. Pope John sprinkled his "salt" on the church little by little, seasoning it to be just so. We too are called to play that role today, little by little, in greatest charity and under the inspiration of the Holy Spirit.

✧ List those social or religious matters you consider most in need of reform today. What prevents such reform from occurring?

✧ What areas of your own spiritual journey have been the most stodgy? Where have you failed to open yourself up to newness and modernity?

✧ Take a few moments to write down all those things that have gotten a bit dusty in your own emotional or psychological "attic." What attitudes, opinions, relationships, or habits could use a more youthful spirit?

✧ Talk with a close friend about which of the following statements best describes your reaction to modern times:
✦ These times are worse than any before in history.
✦ These times are full of danger for the soul.
✦ God is no longer working through human social development.
✦ Everything is getting better and better for the human race.
✦ We are gradually becoming what God wants us to be.

✦ We should not trust that God works through human experience unless it matches the church's teaching exactly.
✦ The Holy Spirit is guiding people in their everyday lives.
✦ Change is good when it brings people closer to God.
✦ The good old days are lost forever, and nothing will ever be good again.

God's Word

You are the salt of the earth; but if salt has lost its taste, how can its saltiness be restored? It is no longer good for anything, but is thrown out and trampled under foot.

You are the light of the world. A city built on a hill cannot be hid. No one after lighting a lamp puts it under the bushel basket, but on the lampstand, and it gives light to all in the house. In the same way, let your light shine before others, so that they may see your good works and give glory to your Father in heaven. (Matthew 5:13–16)

Closing prayer:

O infinitely young God,
    we know that you are with us
    and that you behold all we say and do.
Grant us, by the grace of the Holy Spirit,
    to be as fresh as you
    in our response to your continuing revelation.
Grant us the spirit of newness
    and the willingness to embrace modernity
    so that in all things,
    you can be served. Amen.

O·P·E·N A·R·M·S

Works Cited

Algisi, Leone. *John the Twenty-Third.* Trans. Peter Ryde. London: Darton, Longman and Todd, 1963.

Balducci, Ernesto. *John "The Transitional Pope."* Trans. Dorothy White. New York: McGraw-Hill Book Company, 1965.

Fesquet, Henri, collector. *Wit and Wisdom of Good Pope John.* Trans. Salvator Attanasio. New York: P. J. Kenedy and Sons, 1964.

Giovannetti, Monsignor Albert. *We Have a Pope.* Trans. John Chapin. Westminster, MD: The Newman Press, 1959.

Hatch, Alden. *A Man Named John: The Life of Pope John XXIII.* New York: Hawthorn Books, 1963.

Hebblethwaite, Peter. *Pope John XXIII: Shepherd of the Modern World.* Garden City, NY: Doubleday and Company, 1984.

Huebsch, Bill. *Vatican II in Plain English: The Constitutions.* Allen, TX: Thomas More Publishing, 1997.

Kaiser, Robert Blair. *Pope, Council and World: The Story of Vatican II.* New York: Macmillan Company, 1963.

Klinger, Kurt, collector. *A Pope Laughs: Stories of John XXIII.* Trans. Sally McDevitt Cunneen. New York: Holt, Rinehart and Winston, 1963.

Pepper, Curtis Bill. *An Artist and the Pope.* New York: Grosset and Dunlap, 1968.

Pope John XXIII. *The Encyclicals and Other Messages of John XXIII.* Eds. the staff of *The Pope Speaks* magazine. Washington, DC: TPS Press, 1964.

———. *Journal of a Soul.* Trans. Dorothy White. New York: McGraw-Hill Book Company, 1965.

Titles in the Companions for the Journey Series

Praying with Anthony of Padua

Praying with Benedict

Praying with C. S. Lewis

Praying with Catherine McAuley

Praying with Catherine of Siena

Praying with Clare of Assisi

Praying with Dominic

Praying with Dorothy Day

Praying with Elizabeth Seton

Praying with Francis of Assisi

Praying with Francis de Sales

Praying with Frédéric Ozanam

Praying with Hildegard of Bingen

Praying with Ignatius of Loyola

Praying with John Baptist de La Salle

Praying with John Cardinal Newman

Praying with John of the Cross

Praying with Julian of Norwich

Praying with Louise de Marillac

Praying with Martin Luther

Praying with Meister Eckhart

Praying with Pope John XXIII

Praying with Teresa of Ávila

Praying with Thérèse of Lisieux

Praying with Thomas Merton

Praying with Vincent de Paul

Order from your local religious bookstore or from

Saint Mary's Press
702 TERRACE HEIGHTS
WINONA MN 55987-1320
USA
1-800-533-8095